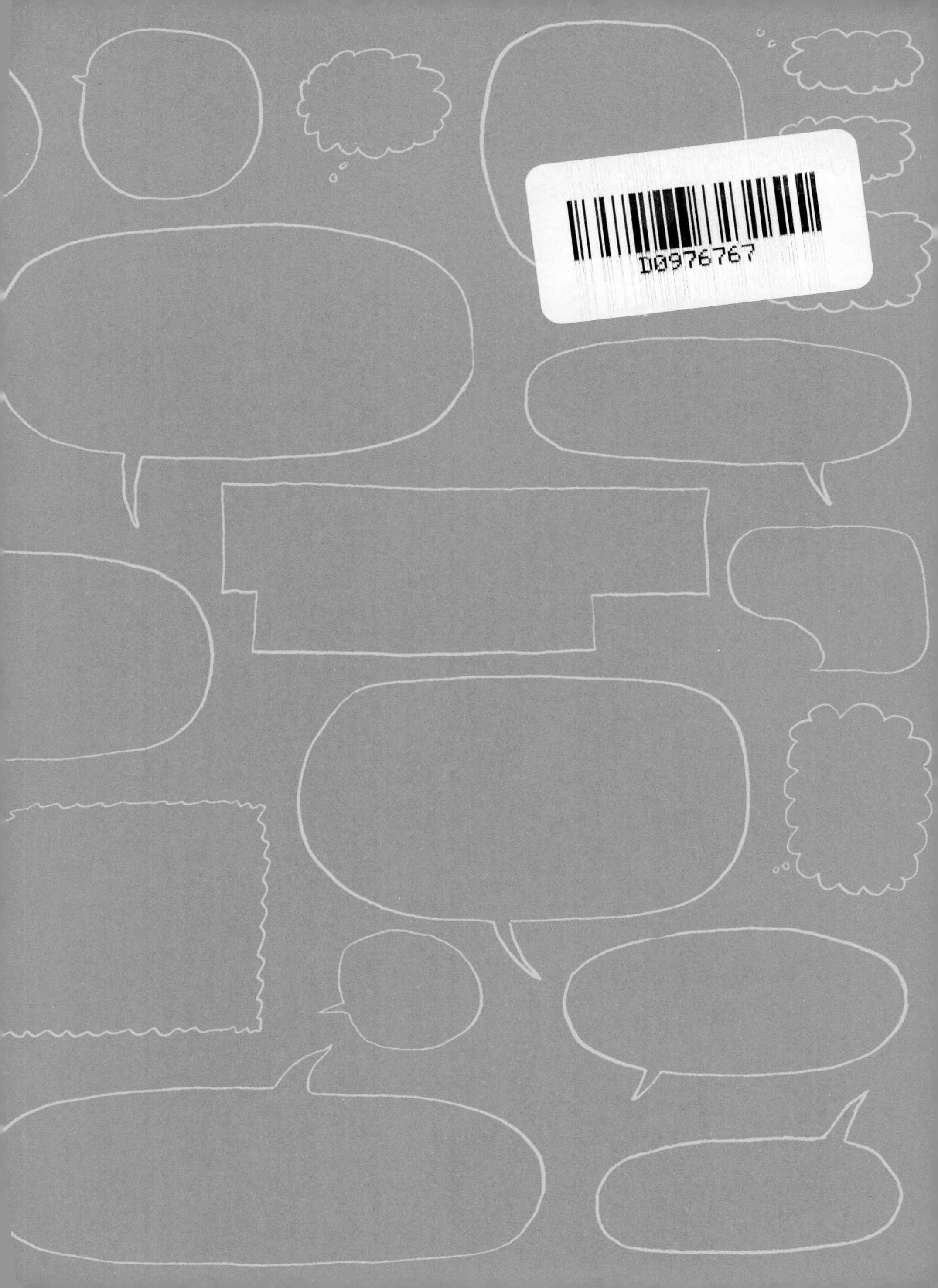

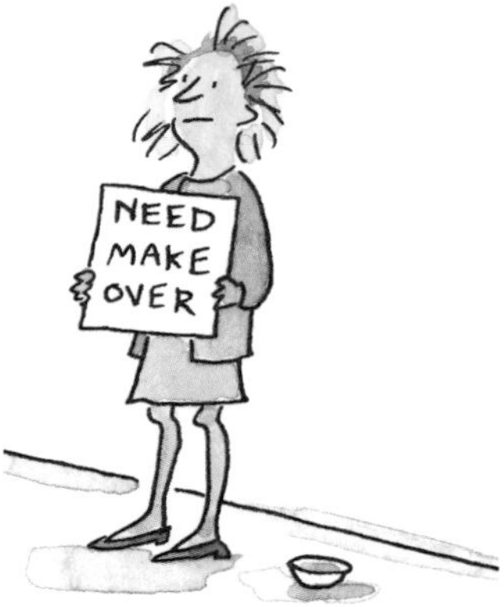
NEED
MAKE
OVER

When Do They Serve the Wine?

The Folly, Flexibility, and Fun
of Being a Woman

by **LIZA DONNELLY**

introduction by **ROZ CHAST**

CHRONICLE BOOKS

SAN FRANCISCO

For my daughters, Ella and Gretchen

Library of Congress Cataloging-in-Publication Data:
Donnelly, Liza.
 When do they serve the wine : the folly, flexibility, and fun of being a woman / Liza Donnelly.
    p. cm.
 ISBN 978-0-8118-7116-7
 1. Women—Caricatures and cartoons. 2. Women—Humor. I. Title.

 NC1429.D565A4 2010
 741.5'6973—dc22

                            2010013385

MANUFACTURED IN China
DESIGNED BY Jennifer Tolo Pierce
Cartoon on p. 6 used with permission of
The New Yorker, The New Yorker Collection,
and www.cartoonbank.com.
Copyright © 1993 by Liza Donnelly.

10 9 8 7 6 5 4 3 2 1

Chronicle Books LLC
680 Second Street
San Francisco, California 94107
www.chroniclebooks.com

contents

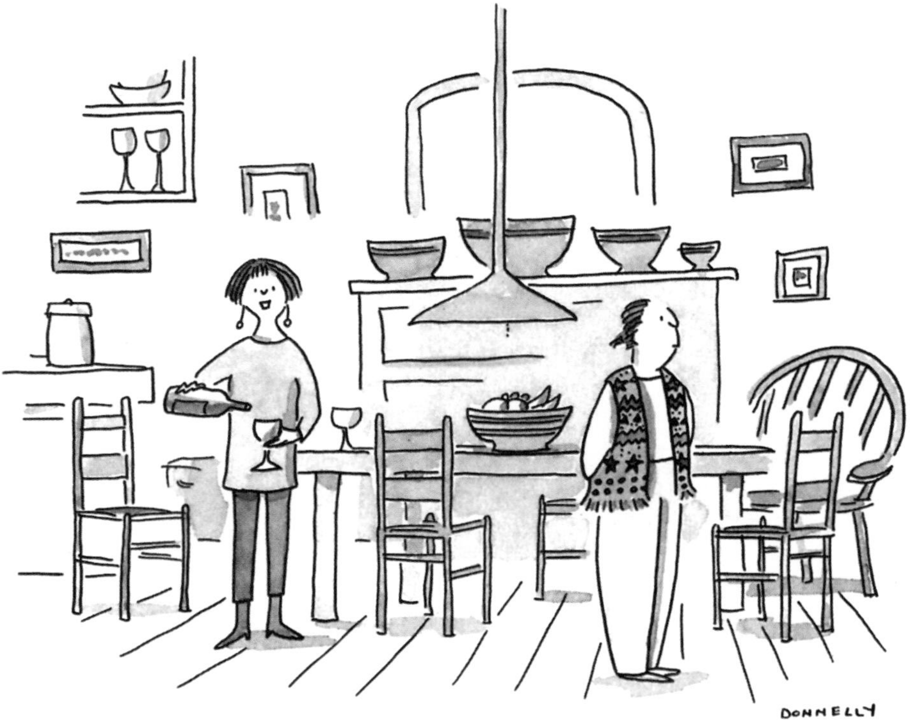
DONNELLY

"Some wine with your vest?"

introduction

By Roz Chast, staff cartoonist, *The New Yorker*

I've known Liza since we were both fledgling cartoonists in the late 1970s. We were in our early 20s, single, and living in New York City in semi-genteel, semi-ramshackle apartments on the Upper West Side. We met while submitting work to *The New Yorker* and, as we became professional cartoonists, we also became friends. We have seen each other through many aspects of life as a woman: dating and boyfriends; building careers from scratch; weddings, husbands, and marriages; getting and being pregnant; living the single life in the city, living the family life in the burbs; seeing our kids speed from preschool through college; and beyond.

I still remember my first visit to the cartoon department of *The New Yorker* quite well. You didn't just walk in there. You had to be invited by Lee Lorenz, the art editor at that time. Unknown cartoonists dropped off their work with the woman manning the little glass-enclosed booth on the 20th floor. If you were invited to show your work, she buzzed you in, and you got to go back to the cartoon offices. The first office is where the editor, Lee Lorenz, worked. Next there was a small office for his assistant, Anne Hall. The third room was where the cartoonists sat on an old sofa or worn wooden chairs or just stood around, anxiously waiting their turns to go in to see Lee. The first time I got buzzed in, I looked around the room and noticed it was all guys. It was also—to my 23-year-old eyes—all old guys. I was not at ease. I wanted to show Lee my cartoons and then escape before something terrible happened. Like, maybe someone would say hello and what would I say back? Or, what if no one said hello at all? Or what if someone asked me what I was doing there. And what was I doing there anyway?

It was World o' Guys back then. Even my son, who had never been to the cartoon department of *The New Yorker*, seemed to have intuited this. Once, when he was not quite 3, I asked him what he thought I did for a living. He said: "You bring your drawings on the train and show them to the men."

When Liza showed up in the cartoon department, it was great just to see another female. I remember she had very, very long hair, and she wore only black-, white-, or off-white-colored clothes. I was impressed that she made unusual, original, and deliberate appearance choices. She was very quiet and serious. But she had a great laugh—a laugh that was genuine.

Of course, those were just first impressions. Over the years, I realized, to my delight, that I had found a new friend. Throughout the '80s, we came to *The New Yorker* cartoon department every week to submit work, and afterward, we went out to lunch with the other cartoonists at grungy Midtown restaurants like Chili, Etc. or The Quiet Man. They made our clothes reek of grease and cigarette smoke. The guys mostly drank beer or the occasional martini or Salty Dog. For a while, for reasons I can no longer remember, Liza and I drank White Russians. Later we smartly switched to the more sensible choice of white wine. We were often—though not always—the only gals in the bunch. But, really, it was no big deal—we were all cartoonists together, and we could all make each other laugh.

One of my favorite cartoons of Liza's shows a man and woman standing in a kitchen. The woman, who is pouring some wine into a glass, asks the man: "Some wine with your vest?" It's a terrific cartoon. Keenly observed, sly, understated, and so, so funny. You, the reader, know that when the guy put that vest on, he thought he looked pretty cool. But it's not quite working out. Plus, he's got that little ponytail. The woman is smiling but not in a mean way. She's really just stating a fact.

This is what Liza excels at. She sees people clearly. She has a terrific ear, and a terrific eye. In this book, she observes us as we stumble collectively and individually through our various milestones, on this one-way trip to who knows where. Liza understands the relationships we have with our friends, our spouses, our parents, and our children.

It sounds so geezer to say, but it does seem like just yesterday we were 23 and figuring out our place in the world. And yet here we are, still drawing. And of course still trying to figure out our place in the world. In her 28 years contributing to *The New Yorker*, Liza's line has been light and agile. In her inimitable deadpan style, she describes the hurdles and hoops we jump over and through at every stage of the game. From the different types of mothers we might have had, to the different types of women we might turn out to be. From our first kiss, to what we imagine sex is going to be, to worrying about our biological clocks, to the age when you look in the mirror and realize that, for the good of humanity, you will never again wear a teeny-weeny yellow polka dot bikini, at least not in public.

To hell with the bikini! Art and humor are ageless. That fact, and this smart book, give me hope.

Here's to humor and creativity, and here's to Liza.

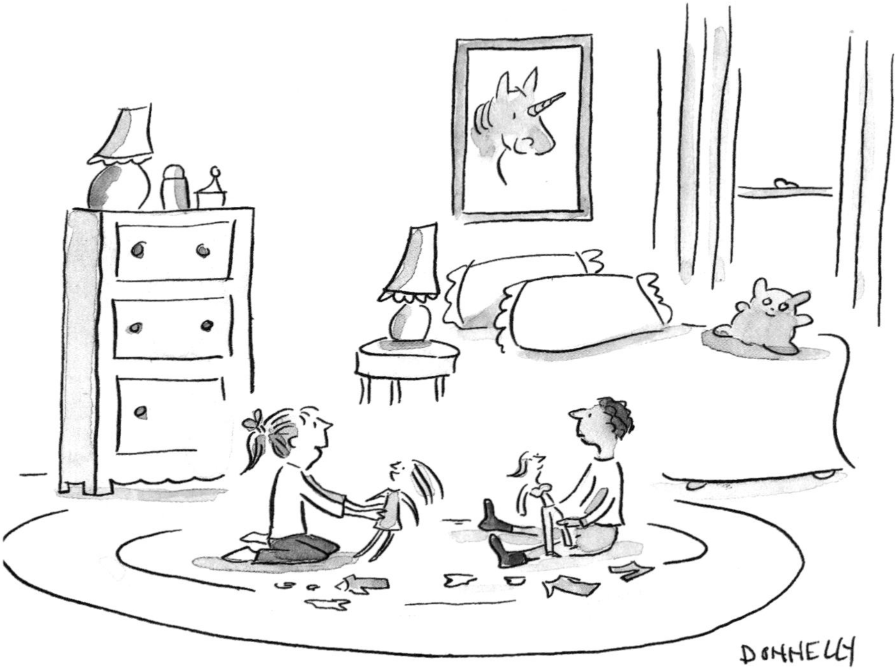
DONNELLY

"I can't decide what I'm going to be when I grow up—a good girl or a slut."

CHAPTER 1

Growing Up

When do you know that you're a girl?

My mother did not invest a lot of money in pink. For one thing, I was her second daughter—and in the beginning, she was busy recuperating from my dangerously early arrival (three months premature!). As loving as she was, we did not do girly things like shopping or painting nails. The only other girl in the house—except for our dog, Sassy—was my rebellious sister, whose tactics incited fear and anger. I quickly learned to be the good girl. Amid these women, it became clear that someone had actually wanted a boy. My father took me to baseball games and taught me golf—all attention I loved. It became a running joke in the family.

At some point, I discovered drawing, and it has saved me.

I learned that being a girl was secondary to my concerns, and I positioned myself quietly on the outside of it all. My cartoons were my identity, and they did the talking/dressing/expressing for me. It has been quite a journey since.

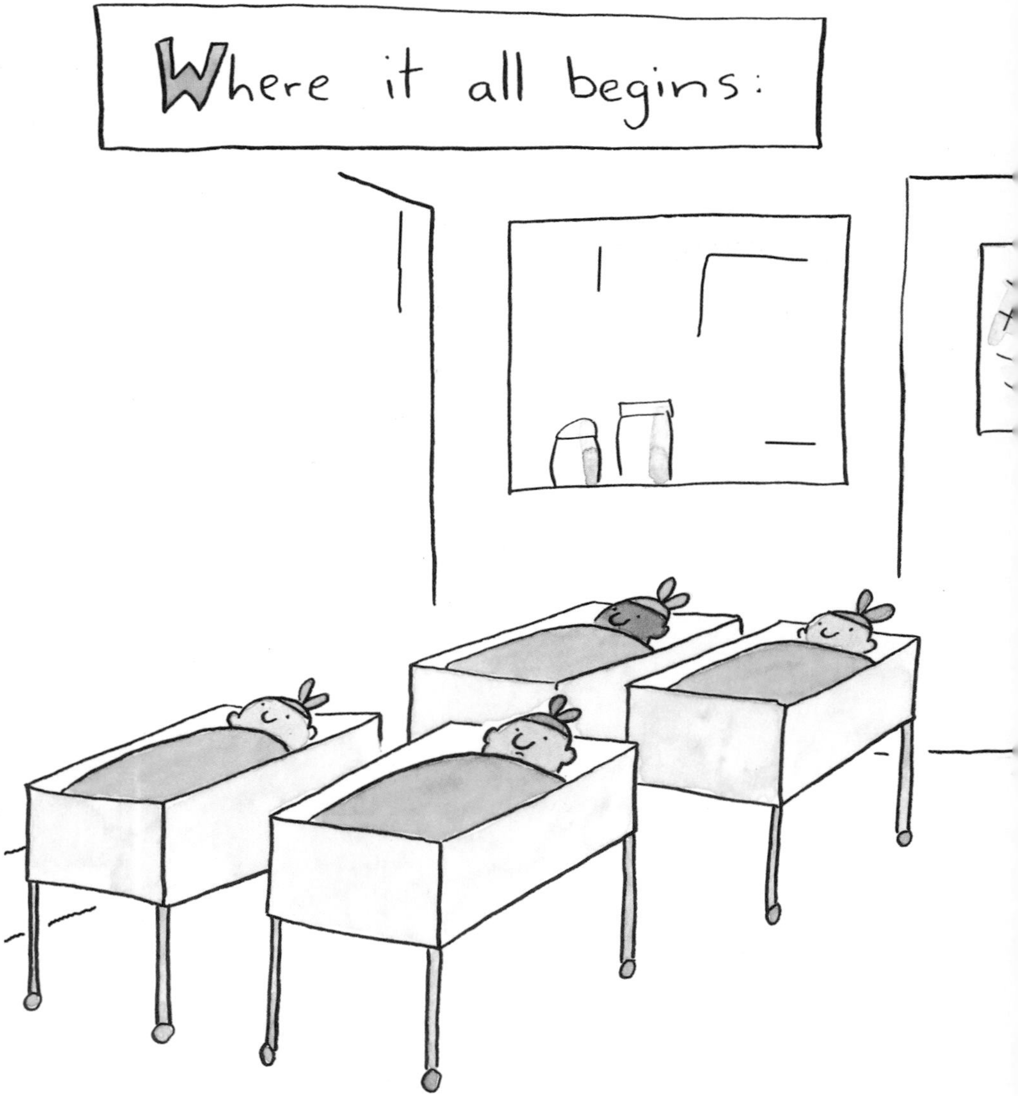
Where it all begins:

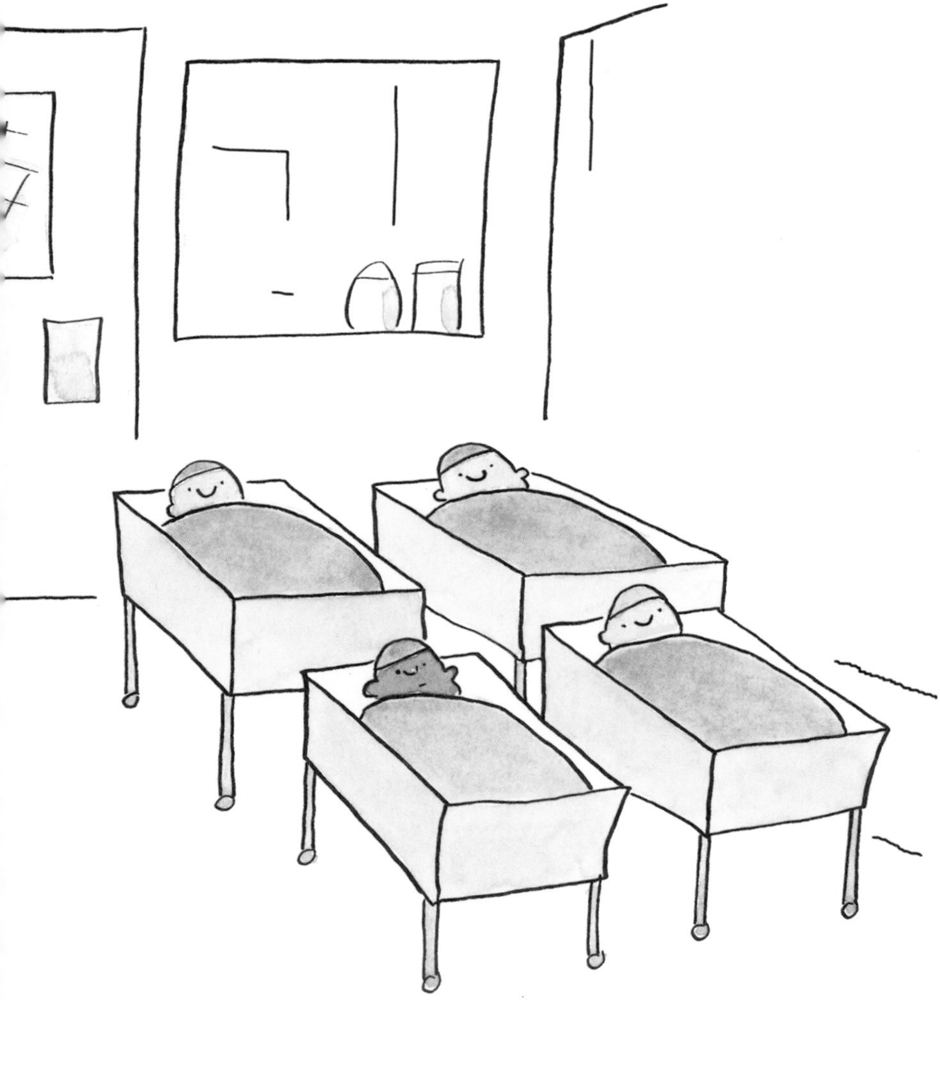

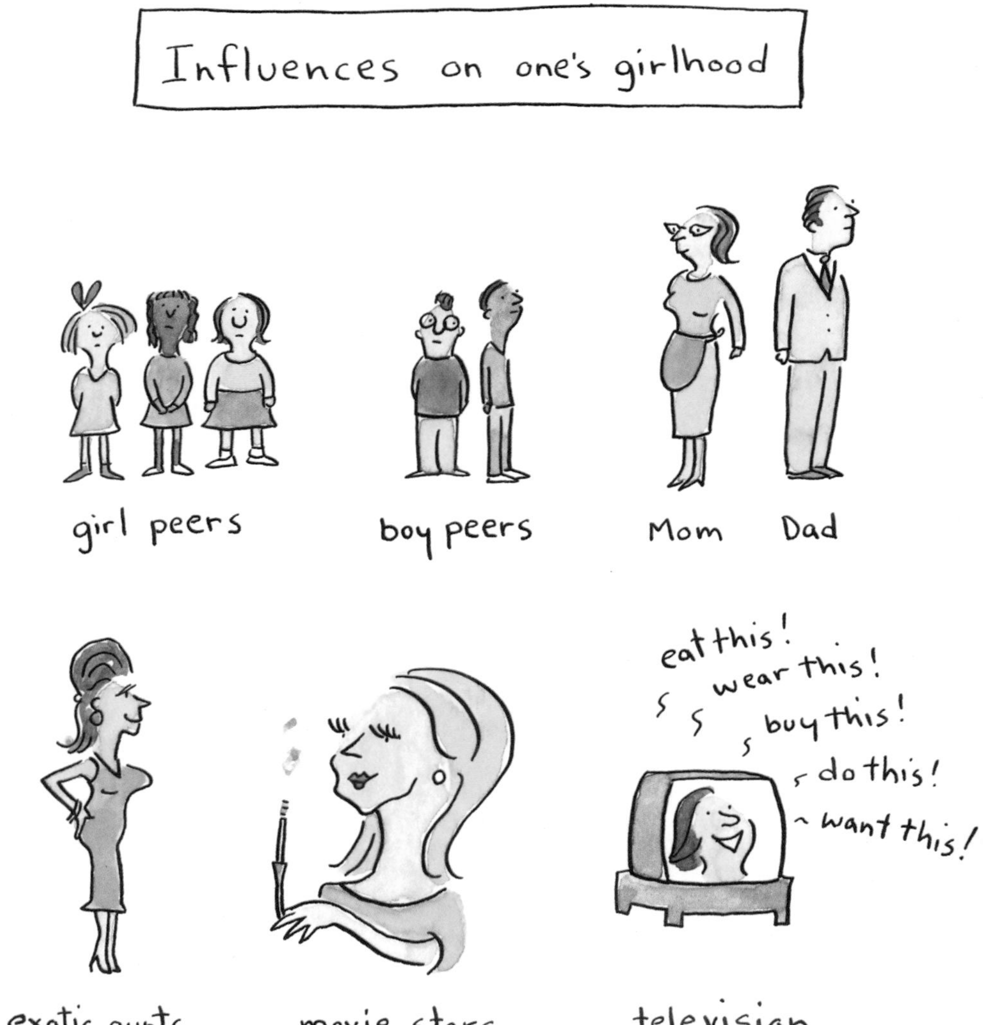
Influences on one's girlhood
girl peers
boy peers
Mom
Dad
eat this!
wear this!
buy this!
do this!
want this!
exotic aunts
movie stars
television

MOTHERS come in Many versions

A.   B.   C.   D.   E.   F.   G.

A. How to make granola
B. How to protest any and everything
C. How to question gender construction
D. the importance of makeup
E. How to be sweet in any situation
F. How to be brainy and sexy
G. How to get the job — whatever it is — done

TRYING on MOM's STUFF

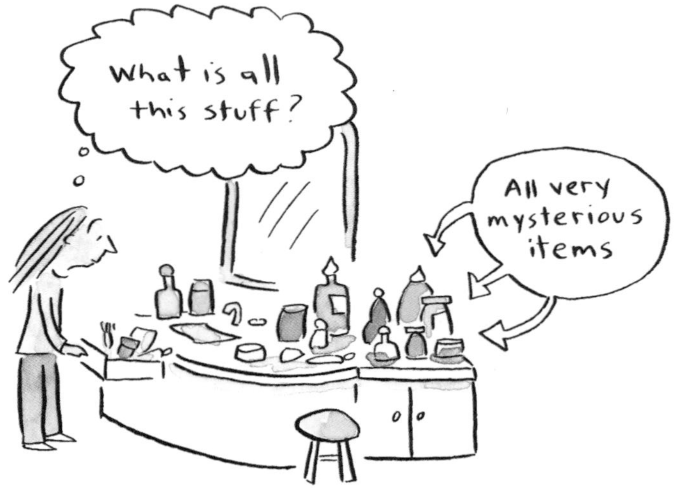
What is all this stuff?
All very mysterious items

So you jump in and apply...

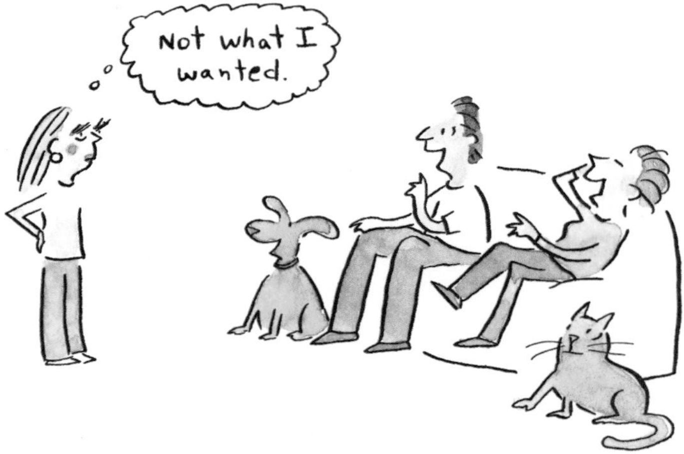
Not what I wanted.

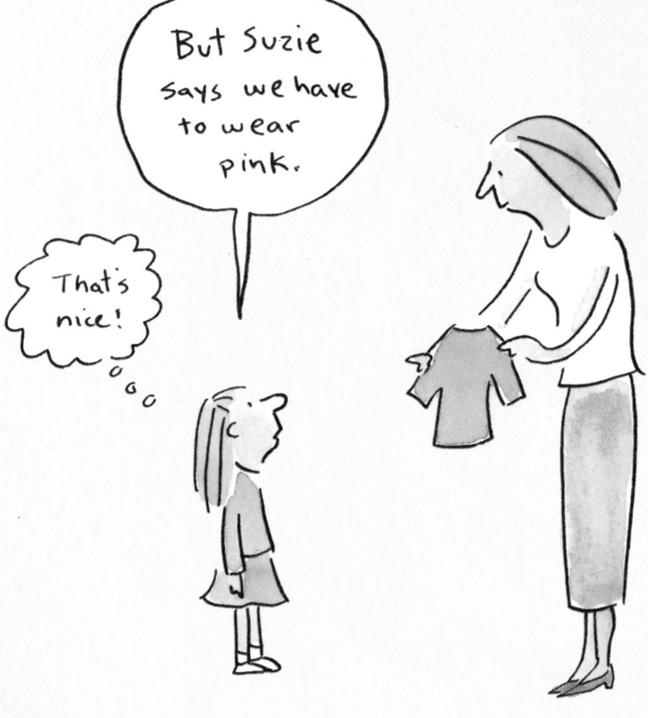
But Suzie says we have to wear pink.
That's nice!

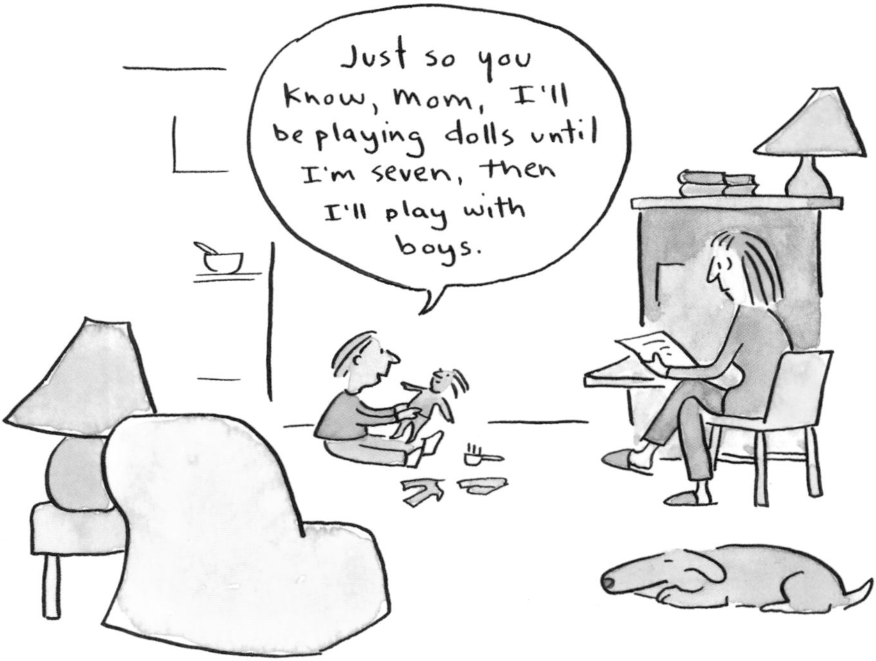
Just so you know, mom, I'll be playing dolls until I'm seven, then I'll play with boys.

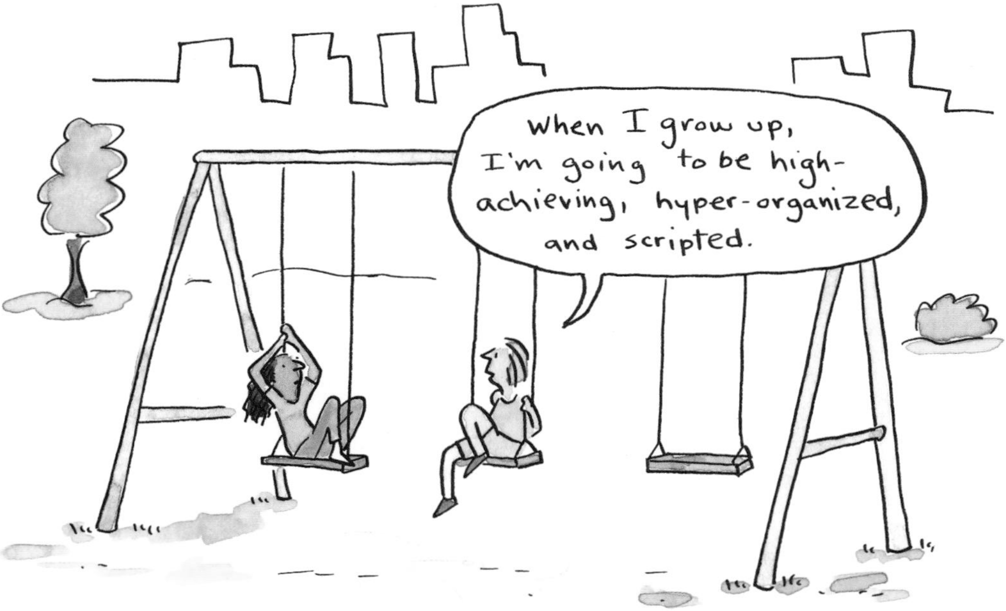
When I grow up, I'm going to be high-achieving, hyper-organized, and scripted.

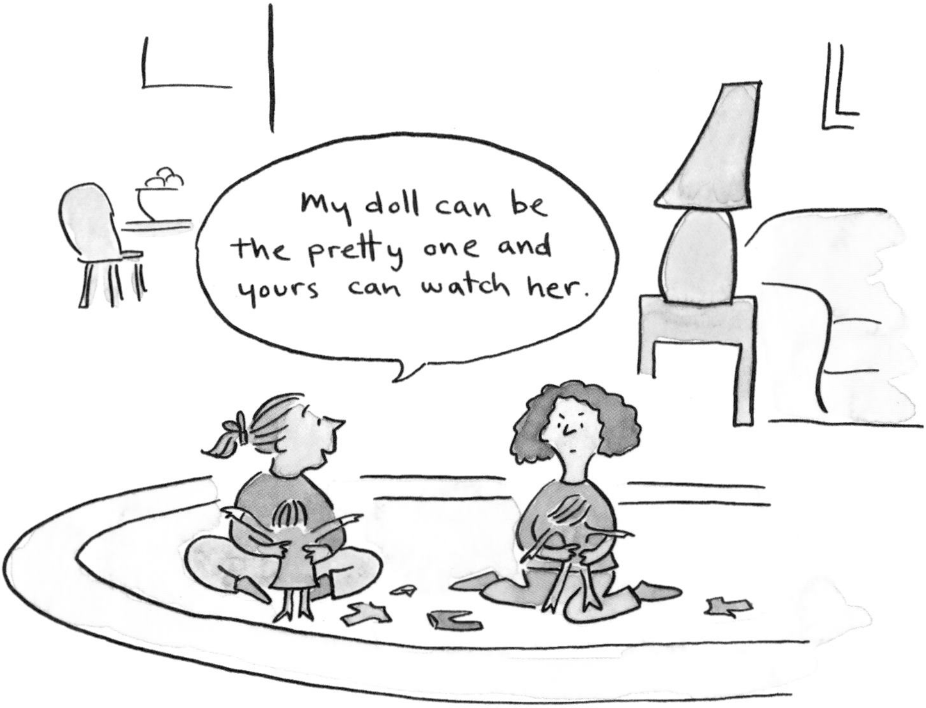
My doll can be the pretty one and yours can watch her.

FEELINGS ABOUT BARBIE

Love
Envy
Hate
Don't
Care

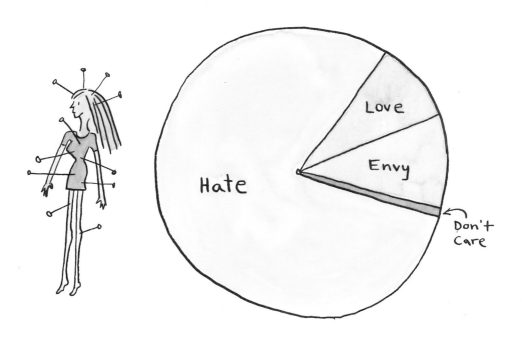

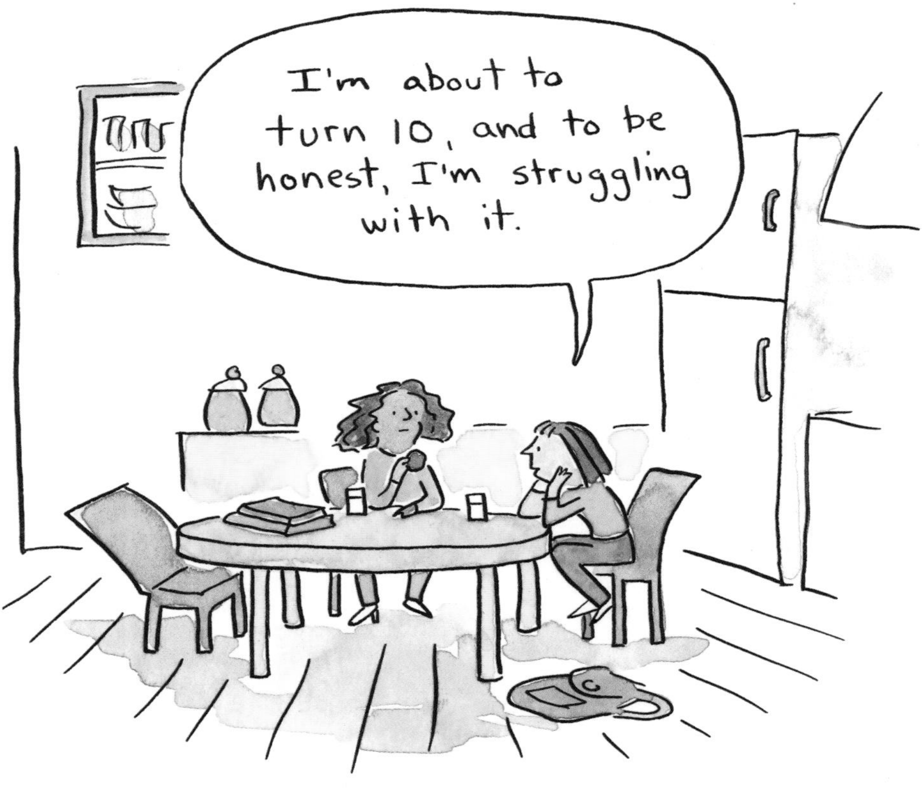
I'm about to turn 10, and to be honest, I'm struggling with it.

If you look like this in your teens, people will assume...

You are an "artist," outside of the box, quirky but creative. You won't be dragged into drama because kids are a little scared of you OR they think you're totally weird.

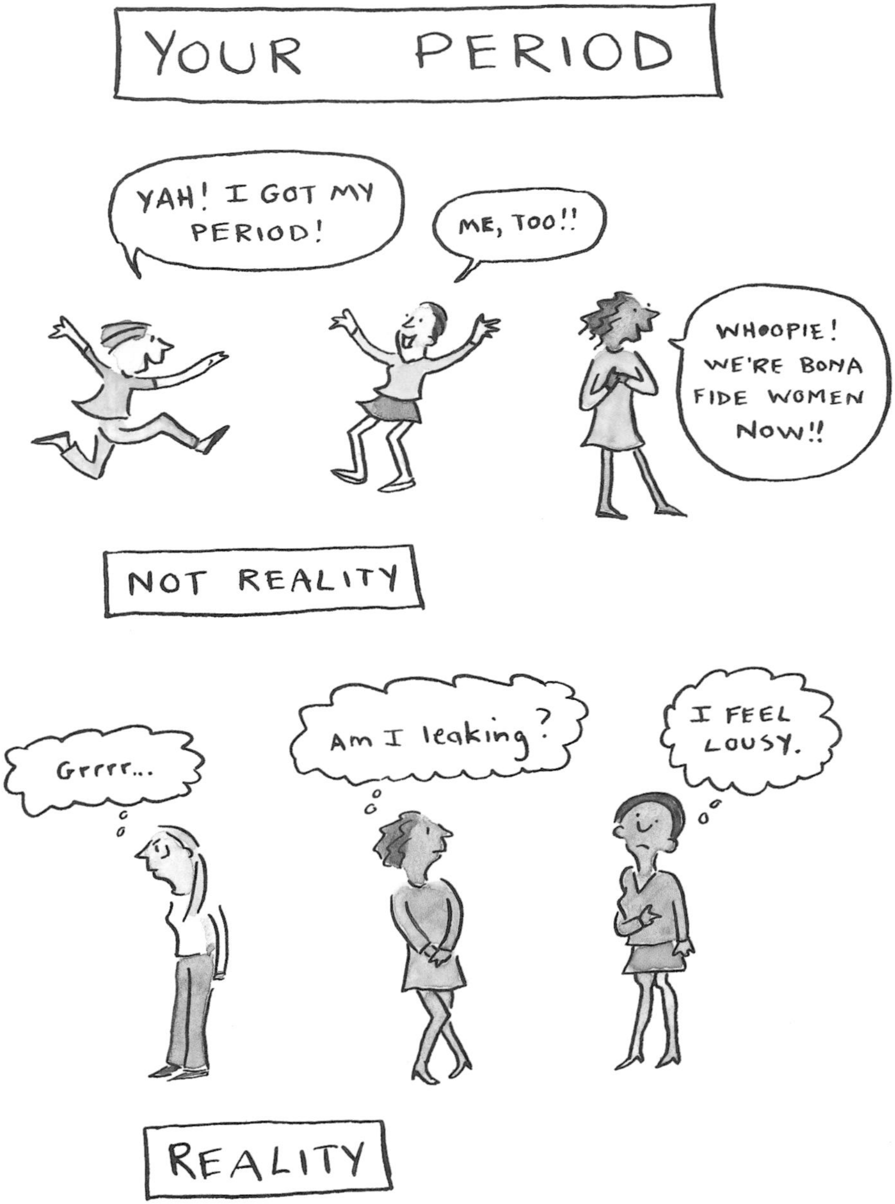
YOUR PERIOD
YAH! I GOT MY PERIOD!
ME, TOO!!
WHOOPIE! WE'RE BONA FIDE WOMEN NOW!!
NOT REALITY
Grrrr...
Am I leaking?
I FEEL LOUSY.
REALITY

HAIRSTYLES to avoid IN HIGH SCHOOL

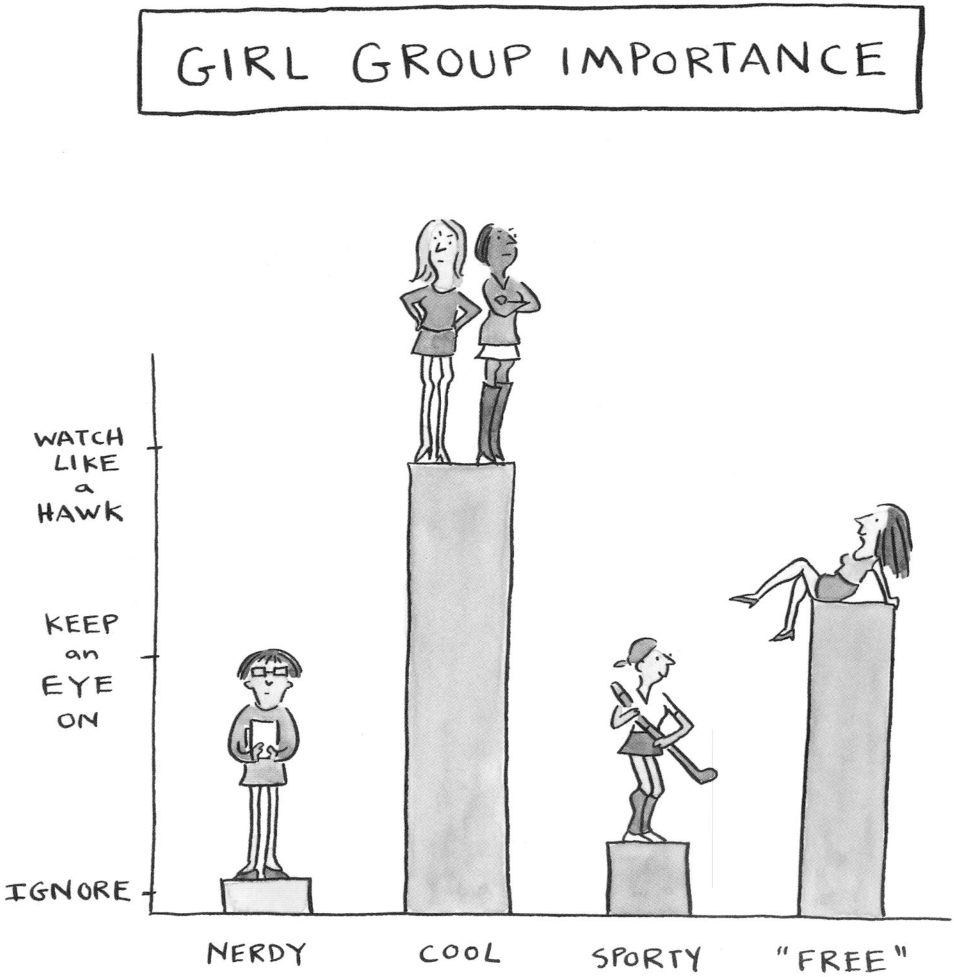
GIRL GROUP IMPORTANCE
WATCH LIKE a HAWK
KEEP an EYE ON
IGNORE
NERDY
COOL
SPORTY
"FREE"

Do you think my pink Miley Cyrus leggings go with my pink Lady Gaga backpack and my pink Beyoncé earrings? Should I be wearing my pink Britney Spears skirt with my pink Paris Hilton tank, you think?

Prom Dresses to Forget

the First Kiss

made you want
to throw up.

confused you.

hooked you.

made you wonder
what hands have to
do with a kiss.

Things you wish you had said in High School.
Enjoy being Miss Perfect now because it's all downhill for you after this.
You are so hot, I just want to eat you up.

Things said that freaked you out (but you didn't let on).

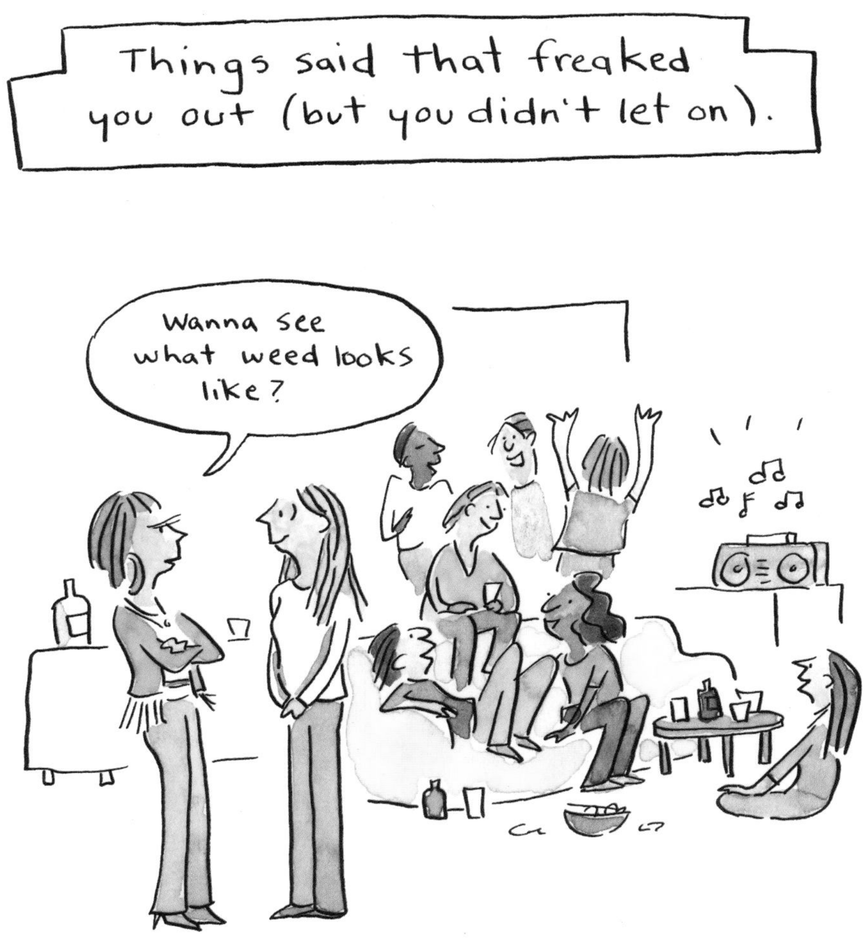

Wanna see what weed looks like?

What is sex?

Fun!
Icky, not for me.
Scary. Go away.
huh?
rebellious (don't like it but it's forbidden, so...)

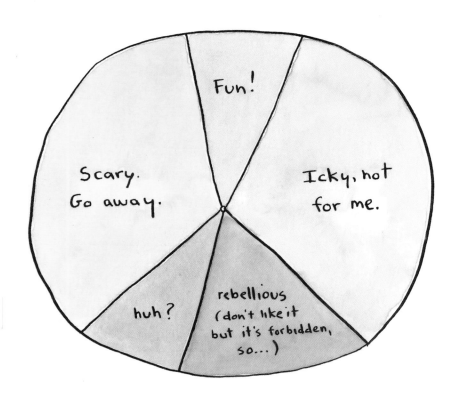

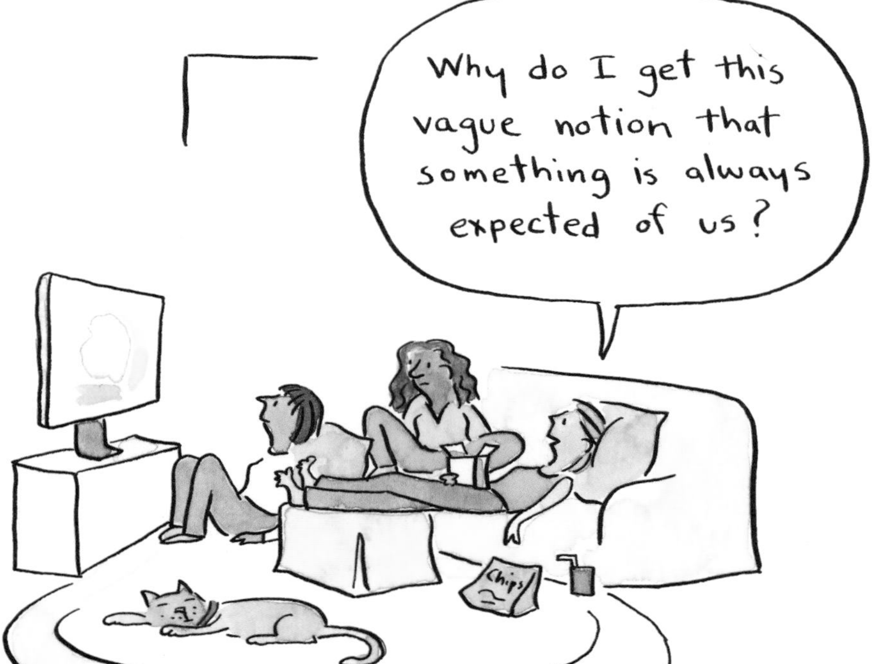
Why do I get this vague notion that something is always expected of us?
Chips

*"In one day, I went from tweeting my
oatmeal to tweeting a revolution."*

DONNELLY

When I moved to New York City in 1977, I had really long blonde hair. I mean, down-below-my-waist long. I loved that my *hair* got attention—and it hid my curves, which I had grown to hate. I wore Earth shoes and refused to wear makeup, paint my nails, or read women's magazines. It was my rebellion of sorts. But it was also a cop-out. Since my hair said "female" in volumes, I did not have to acknowledge my womanness. But there came a time when I realized I had to cut it.

I had never been to a salon before. Clueless, I just picked one near my apartment. When I walked in, the stylist stared at me with a combination of utter disgust and glee, and showed me to the chair. What happened next was a blur. I had finally "come of age"—in a hair salon.

For the next 10 years, I cartooned and dated. I was finding my voice in what I created, how I looked, and who I was with. I tried to find that elusive middle ground—that perfect mix of smart, creative, ambitious (but not *too*), thoughtful, funny, attractive. I spoke very little, fearful my words would betray my lack of confidence. I dated a lot, and my career—while successful—lurched along. But nothing fit right—I found myself casting aside clothing, men, and cartoons on a weekly basis. It was as if this decade was a time to figure out what I *didn't* want.

One thing stayed the same: I never had long hair again.

LOOKING for a JOB ?

What not to wear:

what not to say:

I'm not sure I'm very good.

I can really kick butt!

I've been thinking how your company needs help. It sucks.

what not to do:

kiss the interviewer.

Do your favorite dance.

what not to submit:

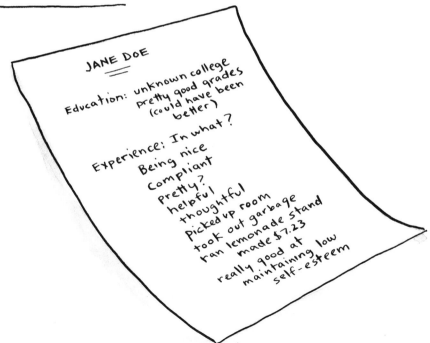

JANE DOE

Education: unknown college
pretty good grades
(could have been
better)

Experience: In what?
Being nice
compliant
pretty?
helpful
thoughtful
picked up room
took out garbage
ran lemonade stand
made $7.23
really good at
maintaining low
self-esteem

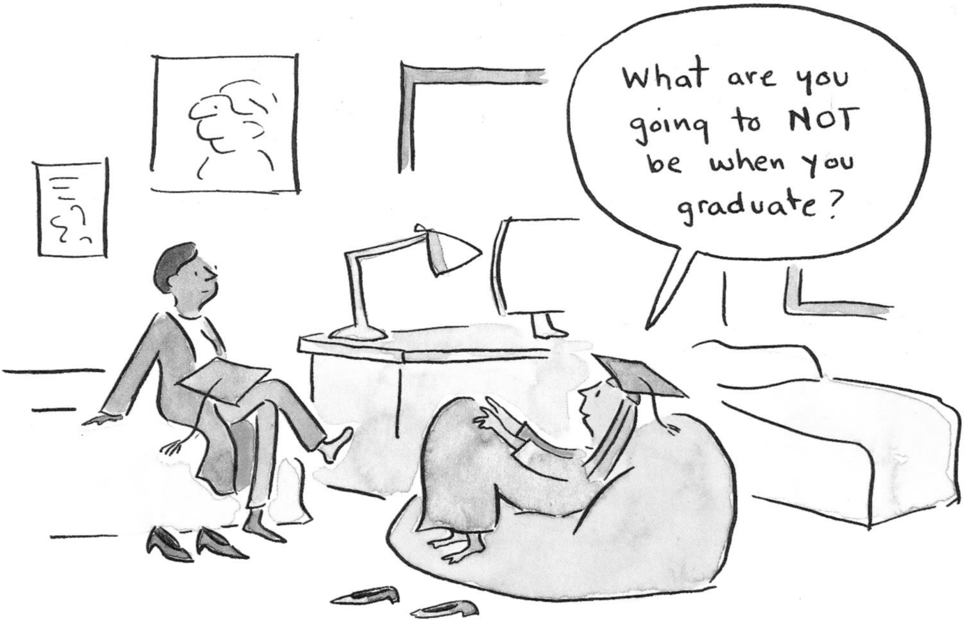
What are you going to NOT be when you graduate?

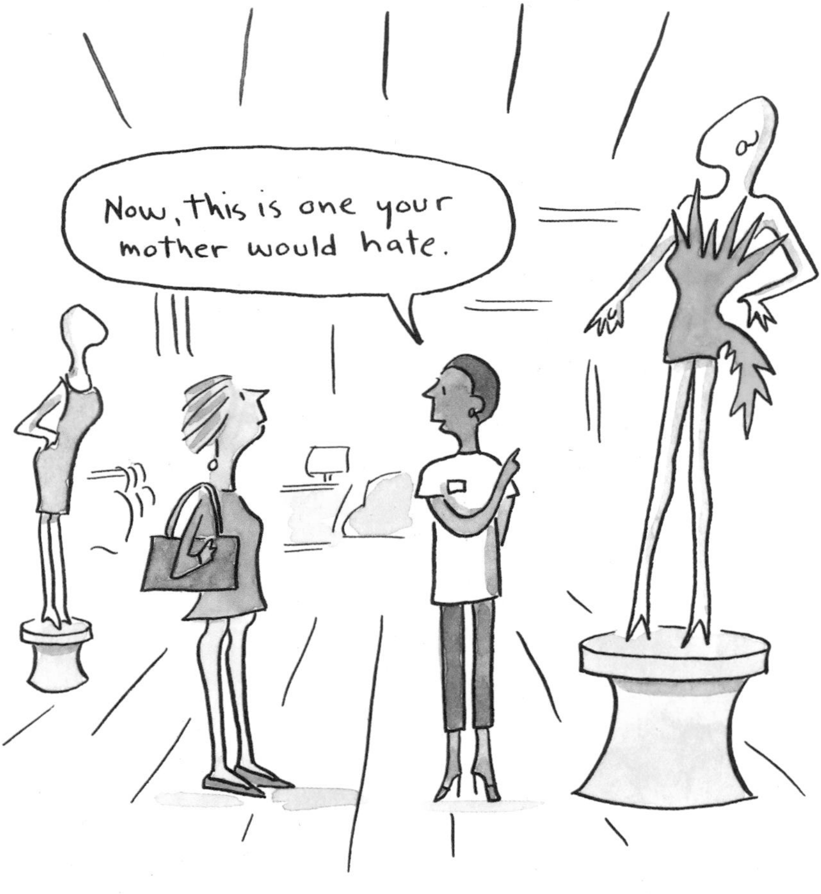
Now, this is one your mother would hate.

Magazines for Women: the 20s

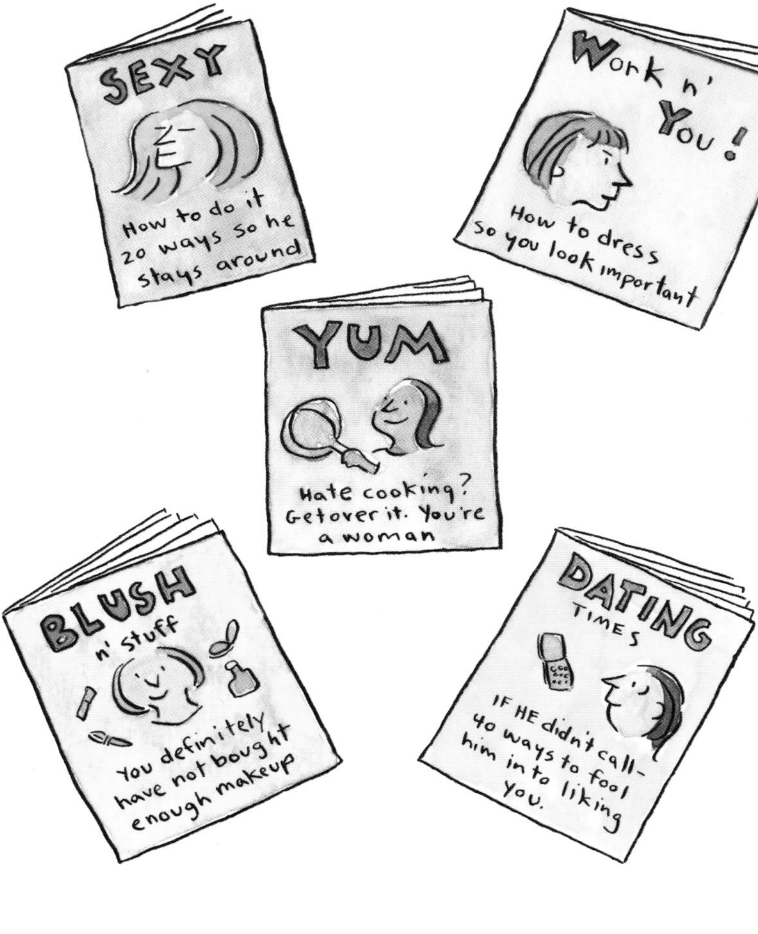
SEXY
How to do it 20 ways so he stays around
Work n' You!
How to dress so you look important
YUM
Hate cooking? Get over it. You're a woman
BLUSH n' stuff
You definitely have not bought enough makeup
DATING TIMES
IF HE didn't call- 40 ways to fool him in to liking you.

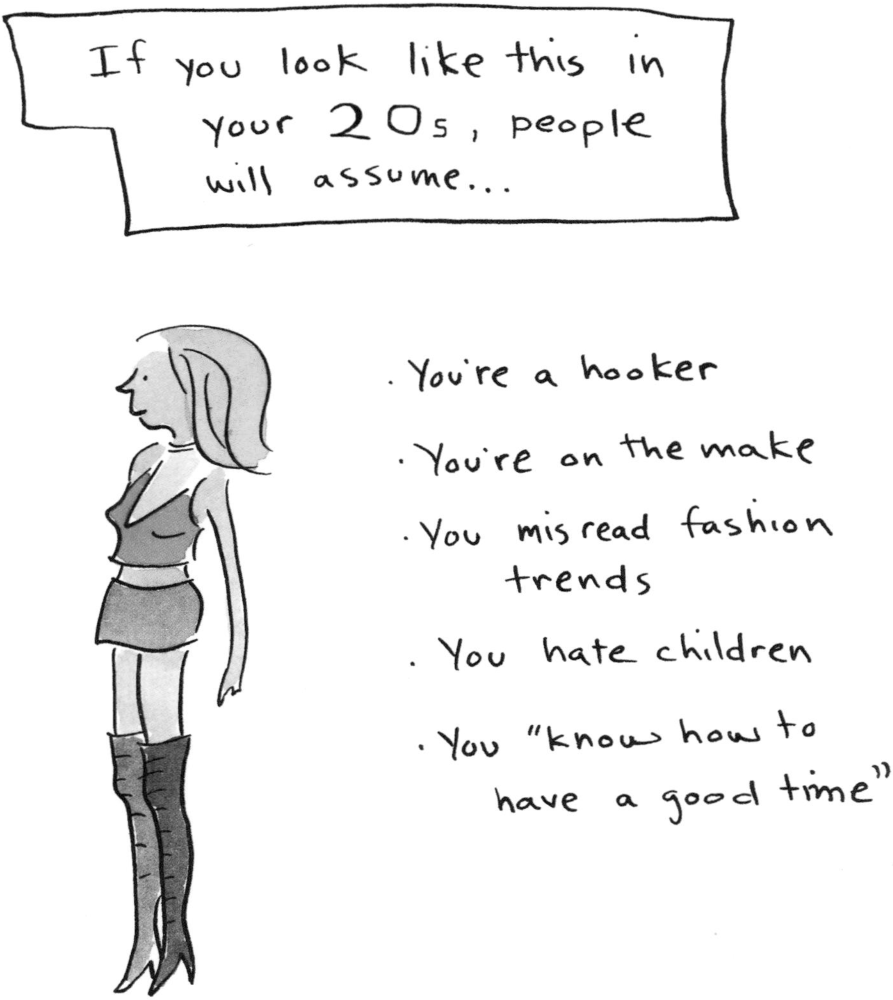
If you look like this in your 20s, people will assume...
. You're a hooker
. You're on the make
. You misread fashion trends
. You hate children
. You "know how to have a good time"

Advice from some first name Celebrity Women

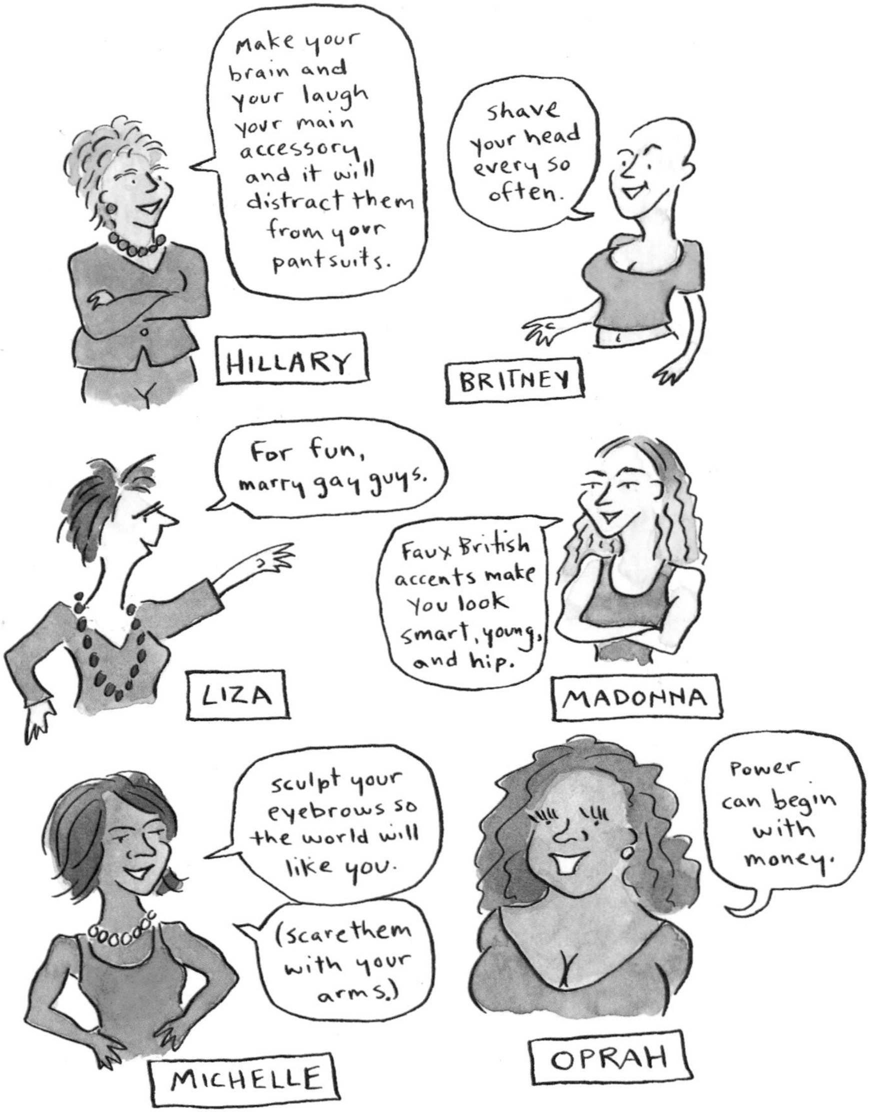

Make your brain and your laugh your main accessory and it will distract them from your pantsuits.
HILLARY
Shave your head every so often.
BRITNEY
For fun, marry gay guys.
LIZA
Faux British accents make you look smart, young, and hip.
MADONNA
Sculpt your eyebrows so the world will like you.
(Scare them with your arms.)
MICHELLE
Power can begin with money.
OPRAH

HAIRSTYLES to AVOID in your 20s

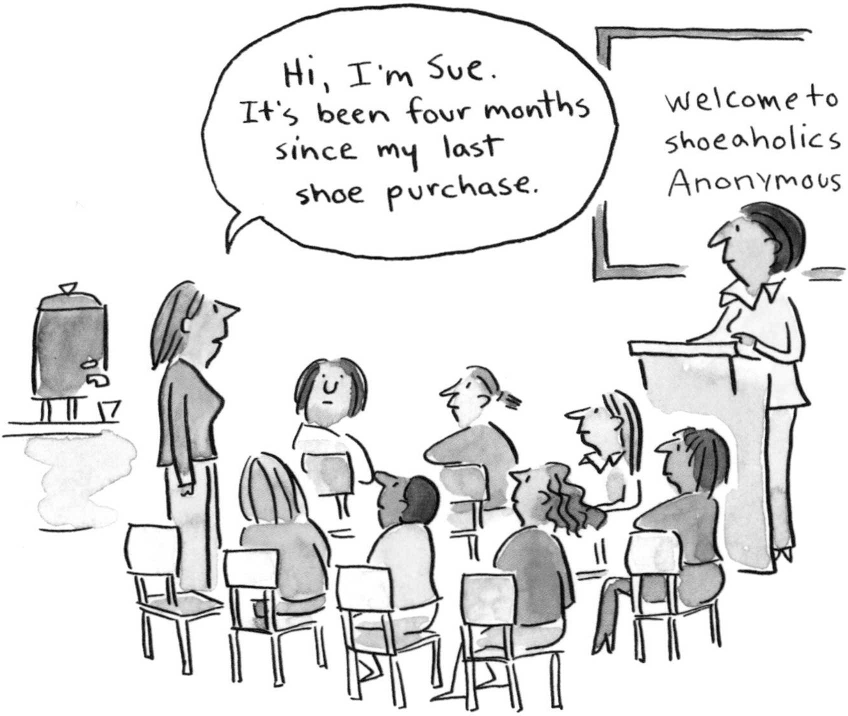
Hi, I'm Sue. It's been four months since my last shoe purchase.
Welcome to shoeaholics Anonymous

Mirror Talk

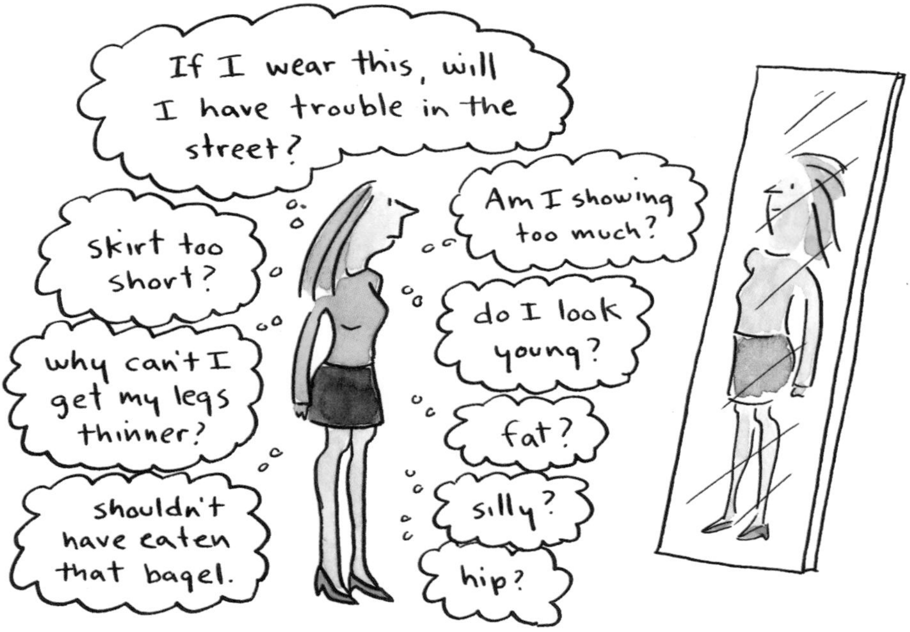

If I wear this, will I have trouble in the street?
skirt too short?
why can't I get my legs thinner?
shouldn't have eaten that bagel.
Am I showing too much?
do I look young?
fat?
silly?
hip?

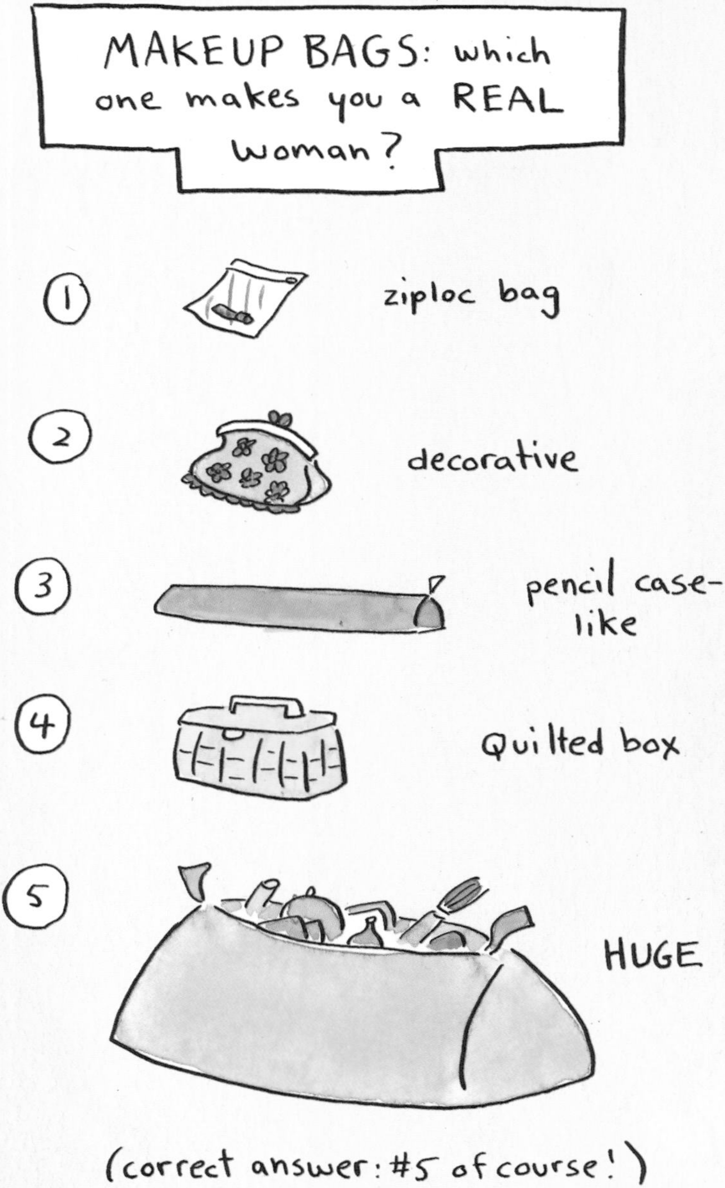
MAKEUP BAGS: which one makes you a REAL woman?
1
ziploc bag
2
decorative
3
pencil case-like
4
Quilted box
5
HUGE
(correct answer: #5 of course!)

BAD-DATE SCENARIOS

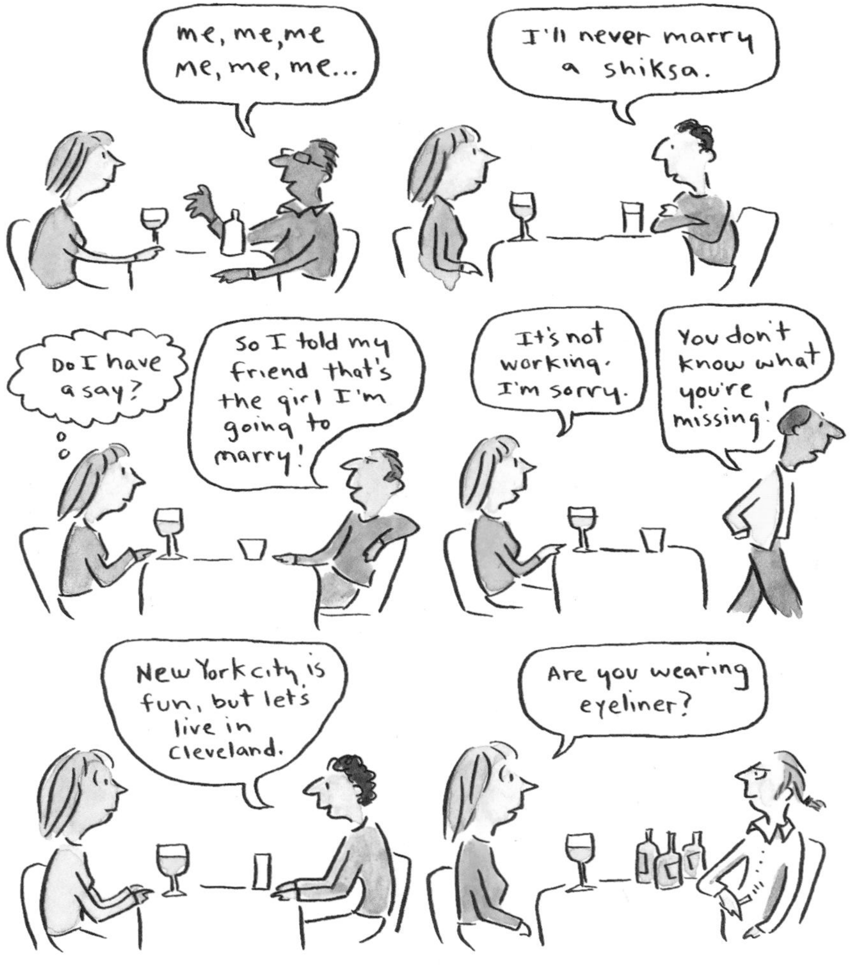
me, me, me
me, me, me...
I'll never marry
a shiksa.
Do I have
a say?
So I told my
friend that's
the girl I'm
going to
marry!
It's not
working.
I'm sorry.
You don't
know what
you're
missing!
New York city is
fun, but let's
live in
Cleveland.
Are you wearing
eyeliner?

When to have Sex

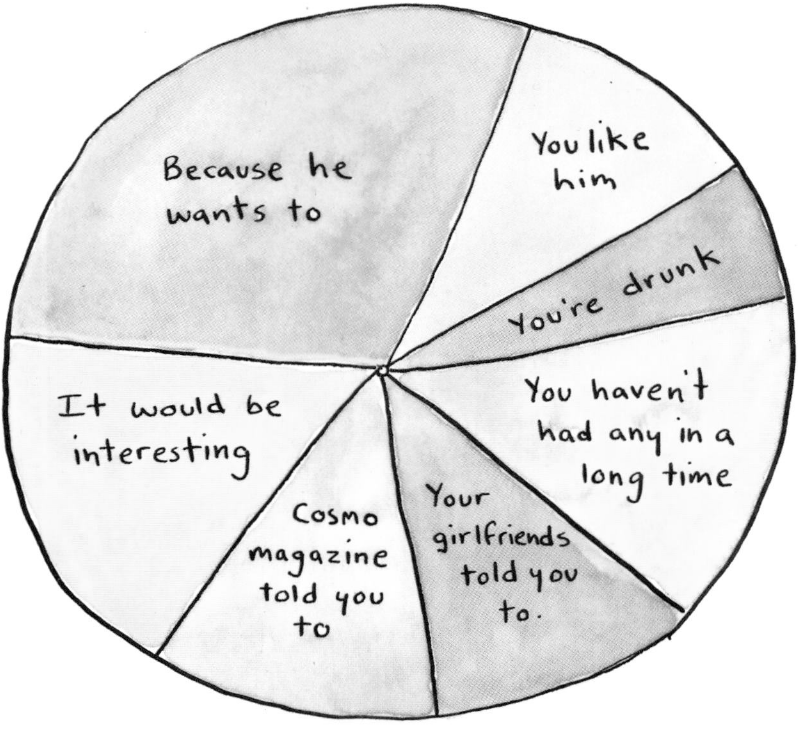

Because he wants to
You like him
You're drunk
You haven't had any in a long time
Your girlfriends told you to.
Cosmo magazine told you to
It would be interesting

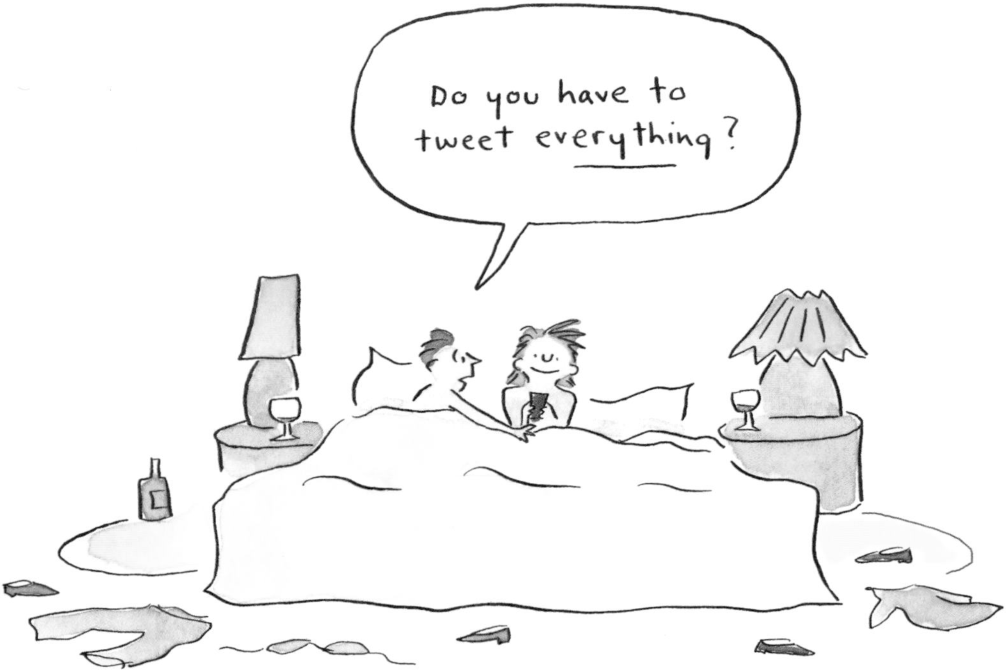
Do you have to tweet everything?

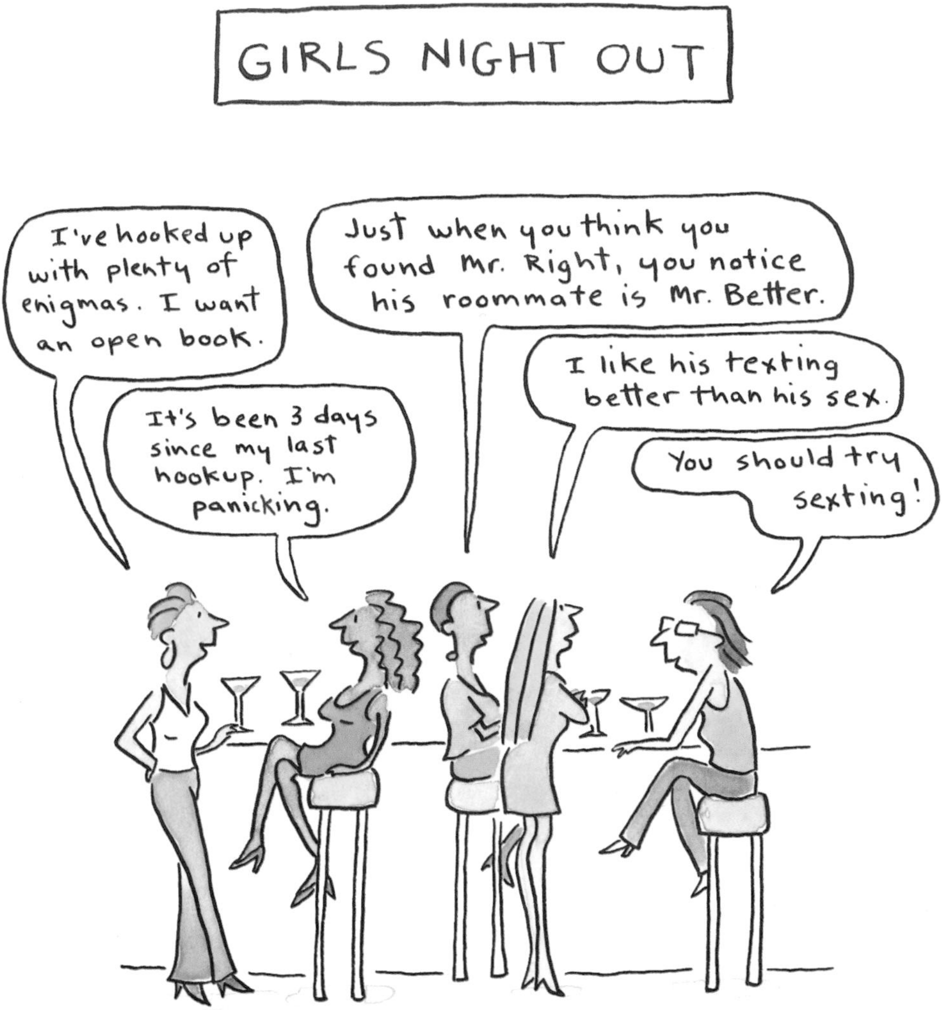
GIRLS NIGHT OUT
I've hooked up with plenty of enigmas. I want an open book.
It's been 3 days since my last hookup. I'm panicking.
Just when you think you found Mr. Right, you notice his roommate is Mr. Better.
I like his texting better than his sex.
You should try sexting!

Sex in the Studio Apartment

Noncommittal Men

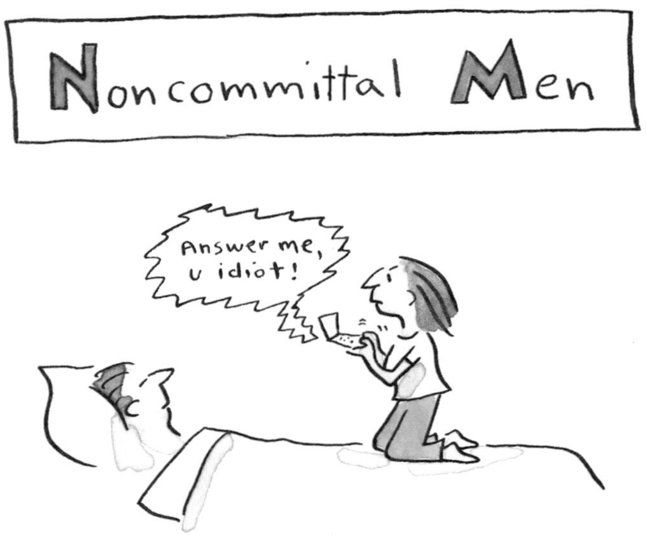
Answer me,
u idiot!

He won't commit to answering your texts.

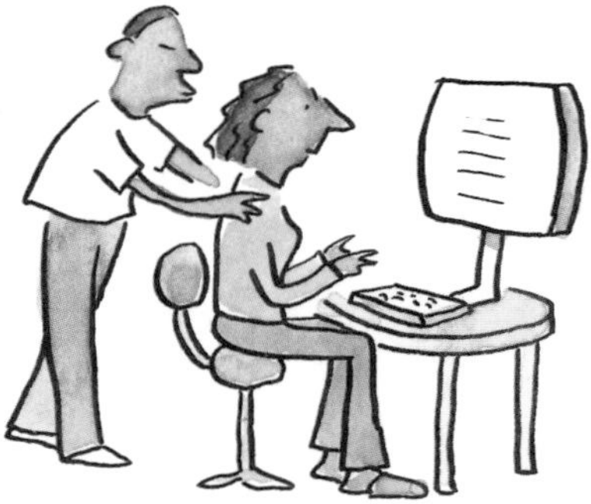

He won't commit to letting you work.

EVERYONE'S DOING IT

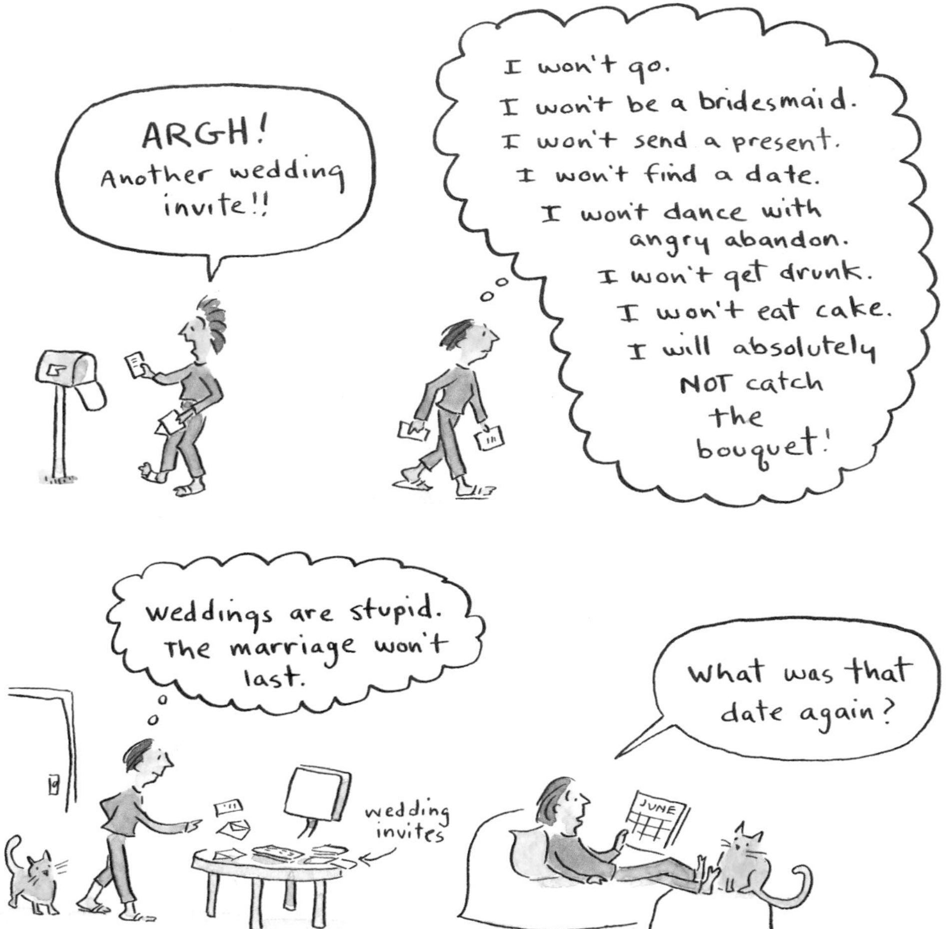
ARGH! Another wedding invite!!
I won't go.
I won't be a bridesmaid.
I won't send a present.
I won't find a date.
I won't dance with angry abandon.
I won't get drunk.
I won't eat cake.
I will absolutely NOT catch the bouquet!
weddings are stupid. The marriage won't last.
wedding invites
JUNE
What was that date again?

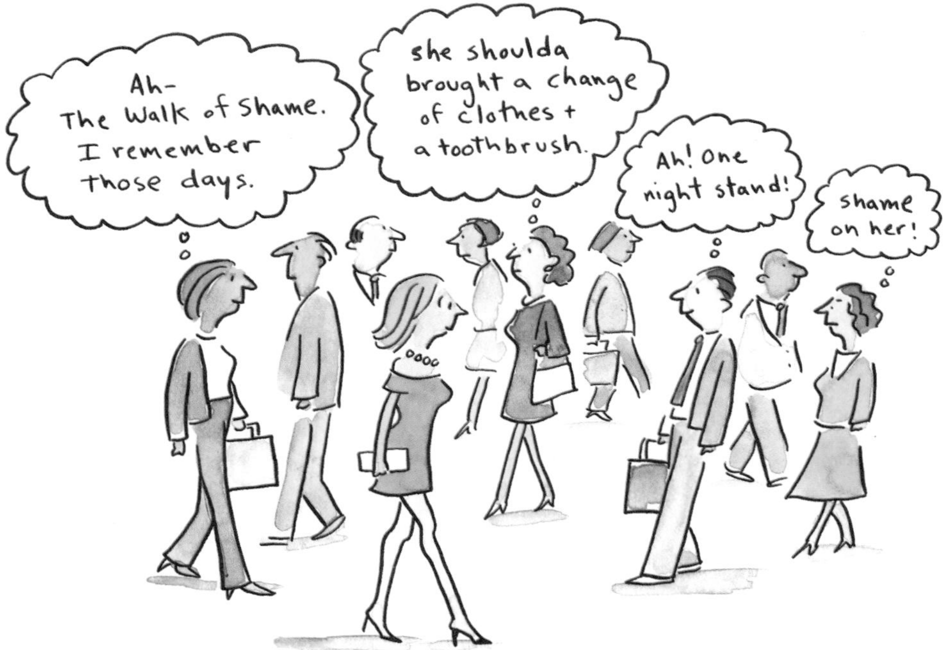
Ah-
The Walk of Shame.
I remember
those days.
she shoulda
brought a change
of clothes +
a toothbrush.
Ah! One
night stand!
shame
on her!

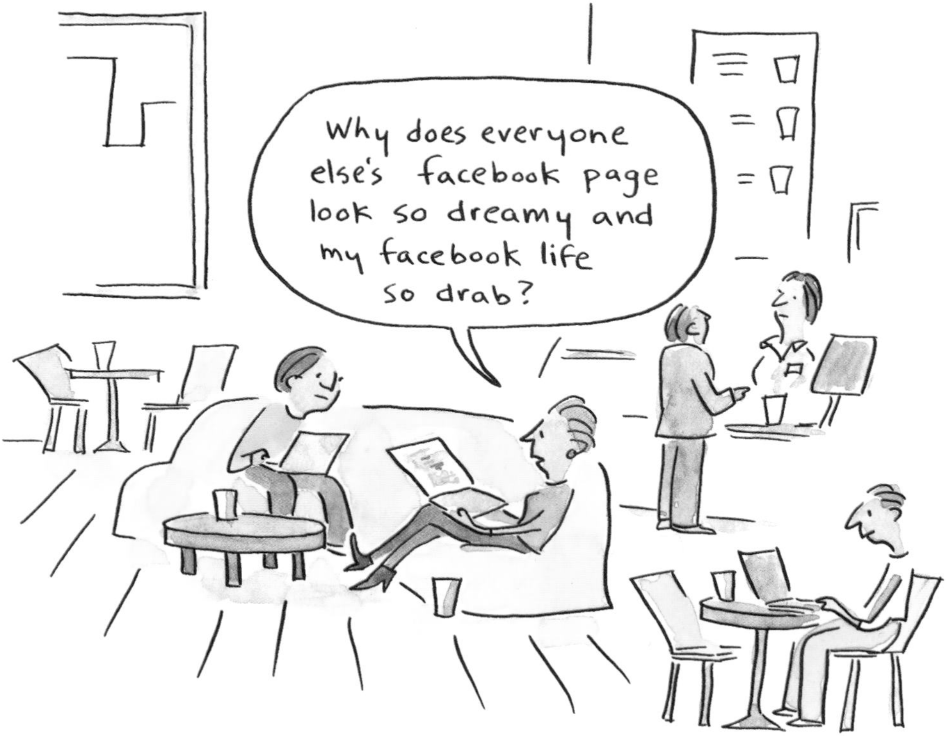
Why does everyone else's facebook page look so dreamy and my facebook life so drab?

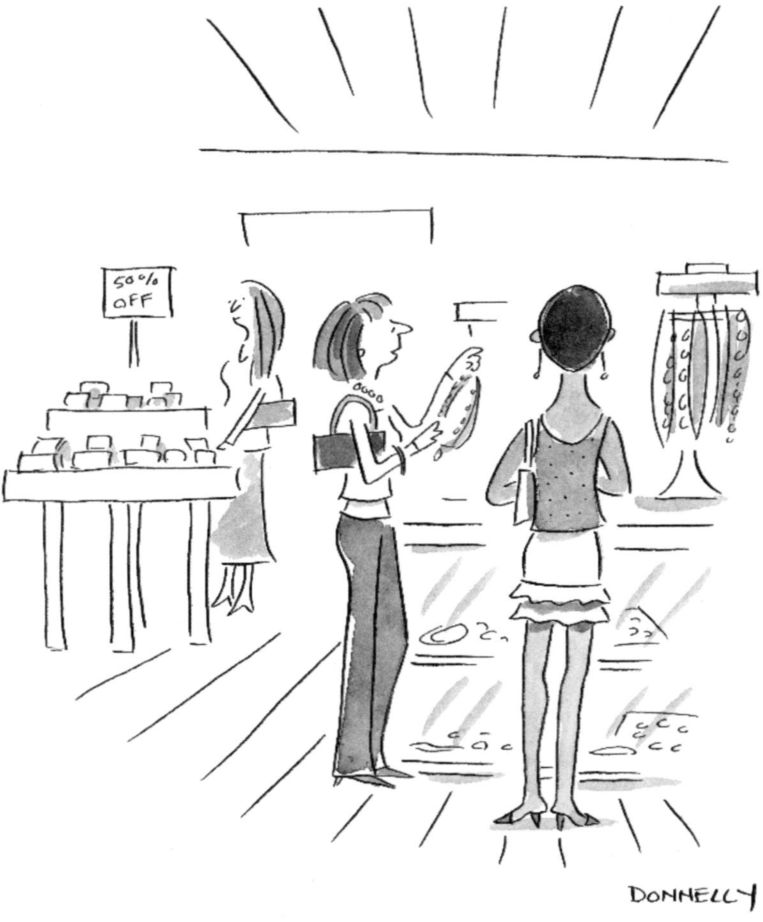
50%
OFF
DONNELLY

"Some of my best friends are married."

CHAPTER 3

30s

When I turned 30, I threw myself a party. I invited all my friends. I even took a chance and invited a man I had met recently, a fellow cartoonist for *The New Yorker*. As it turned out, he couldn't come.

Marriage had been on my mind. I had decided to accept the idea of marriage for myself. I had expected to get married by 28. It seemed reasonable. But there were a few problems. The men I dated were either noncommittal, incommunicative, wore strange clothing, chewed with their mouths open, or all of the above. And I was trying too hard to mold myself to them. It seemed I didn't know myself anymore, much less what I wanted. My shrink suggested—news flash—that maybe it had something to do with my parents' divorce. But like a good shrink, she offered no concrete prescription, so I kept on going.

Just when I thought I was destined to be the stereotypic lonely, pathetic, angry, man-hating, children-hating, cranky, frumpy, "eccentric" old maid, things changed. The man who couldn't come to my 30th birthday party entered my life four years later—and we got married. We had finally found each other. How did I know it was right? Maybe I needed to have all those boyfriends, or maybe those extra four years made the difference. Maybe it was simply the feeling that I was myself again.

USE NEW ADJECTIVES for YOURSELF

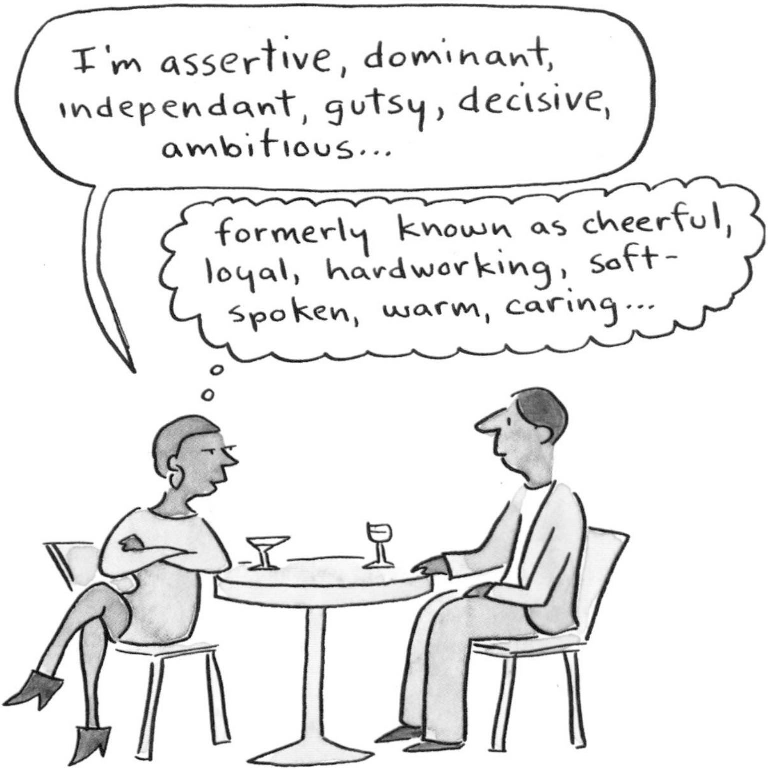
I'm assertive, dominant, independant, gutsy, decisive, ambitious...
formerly known as cheerful, loyal, hardworking, soft-spoken, warm, caring...

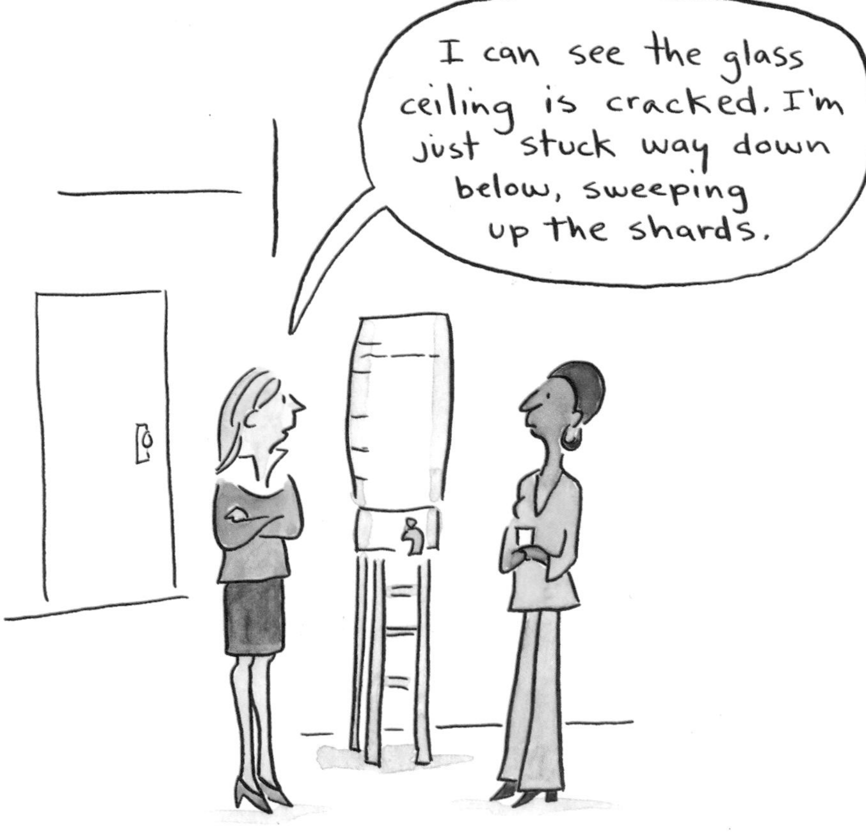
I can see the glass ceiling is cracked. I'm just stuck way down below, sweeping up the shards.

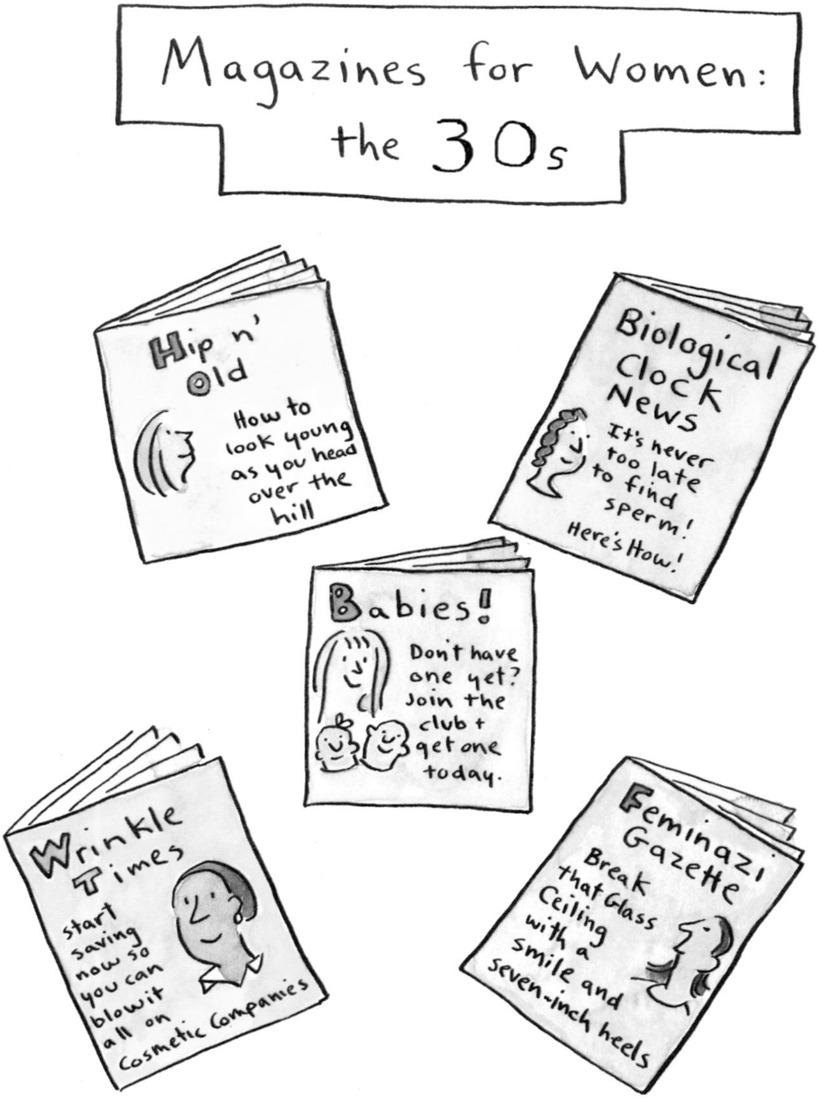

Magazines for Women: the 30s
Hip n' Old
How to look young as you head over the hill
Biological Clock News
It's never too late to find sperm! Here's How!
Babies!
Don't have one yet? Join the club + get one today.
Wrinkle Times
start saving now so you can blow it all on Cosmetic Companies
Feminazi Gazette
Break that Glass Ceiling with a smile and seven-inch heels

If you look like this in your 30s people will assume...

- You are a lesbian
- You are a Fran Lebowitz wannabe
- You are attempting to climb the corporate ladder without resorting to using your sex
- You were a women's studies major

HAIRSTYLES to AVOID in your 30s

What we wish Construction workers would really Say:

a. You look really intelligent!

b. You chose some great color combinations!

c. You look like an important person!

d. They're going to promote you today!

e. You don't look old!

f. We're idiots and apologize for man's insensitivity to women.

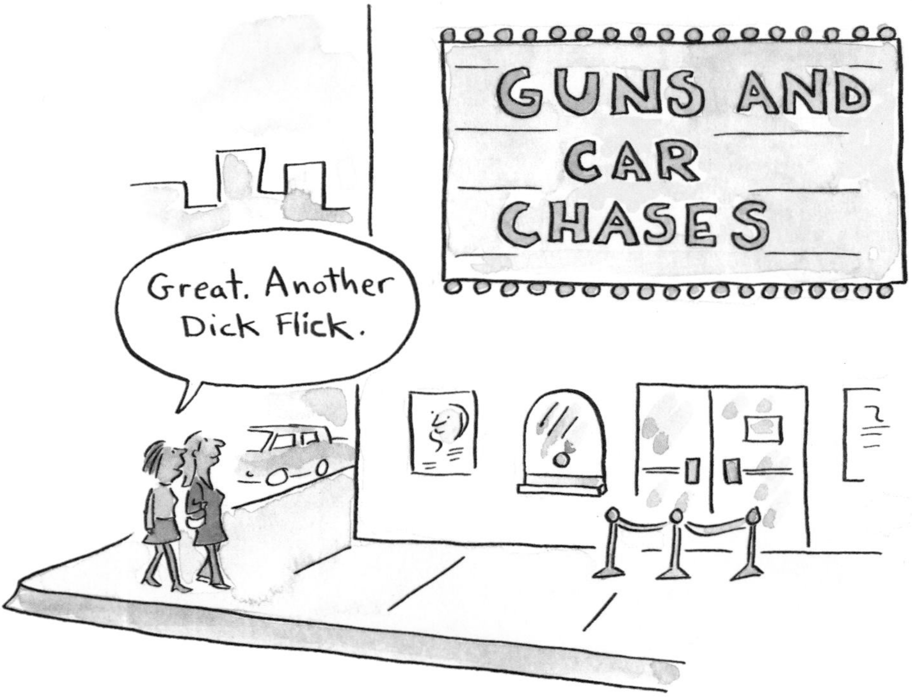
GUNS AND CAR CHASES
Great. Another Dick Flick.

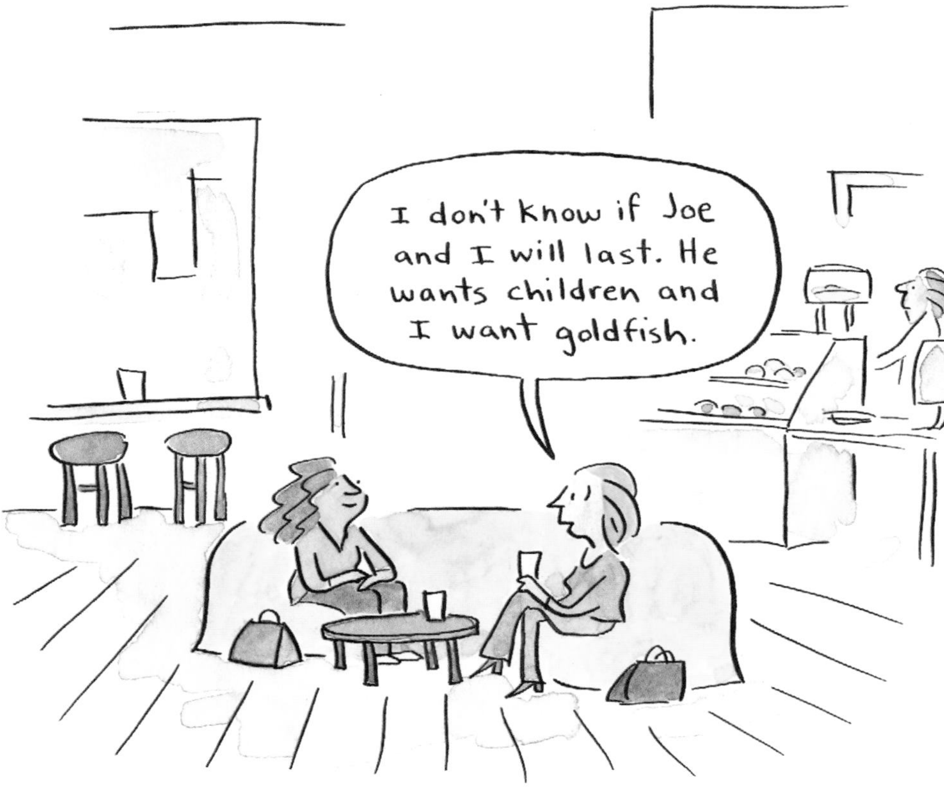
I don't know if Joe and I will last. He wants children and I want goldfish.

Noncommittal Men

He won't commit to either:

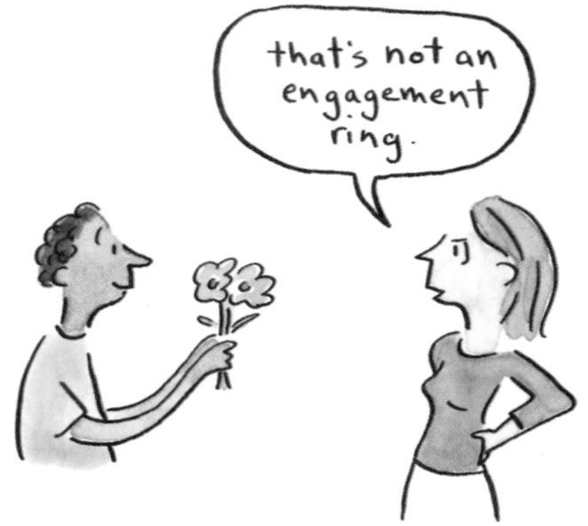
that's not an engagement ring.

a) giving you a rock

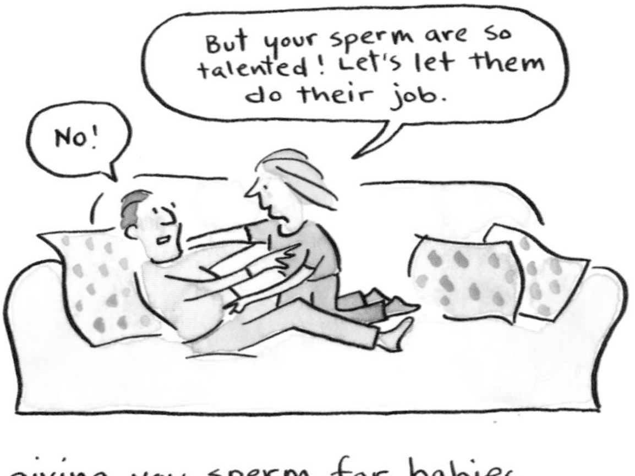
No!
But your sperm are so talented! Let's let them do their job.

b) giving you sperm for babies
(he wants it to go to waste!)

where to find a mate

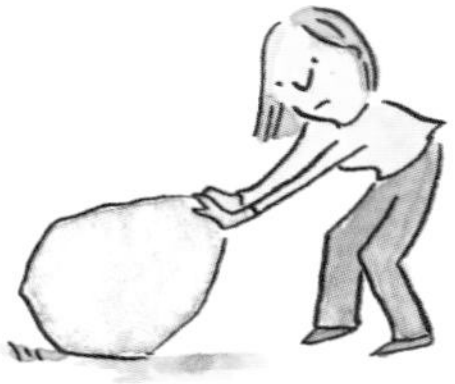

under a rock?

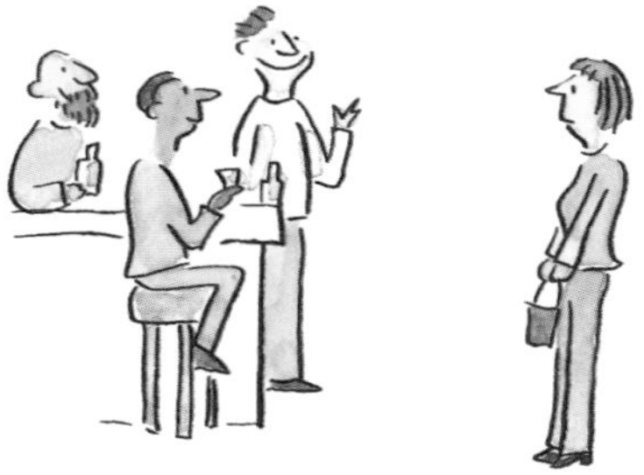

in a bar?

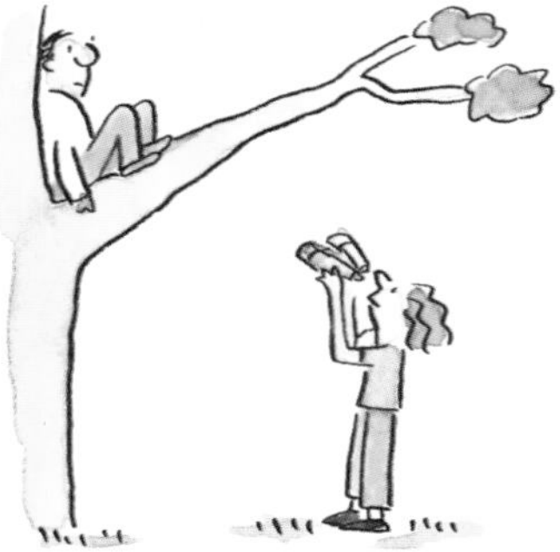

in a tree?

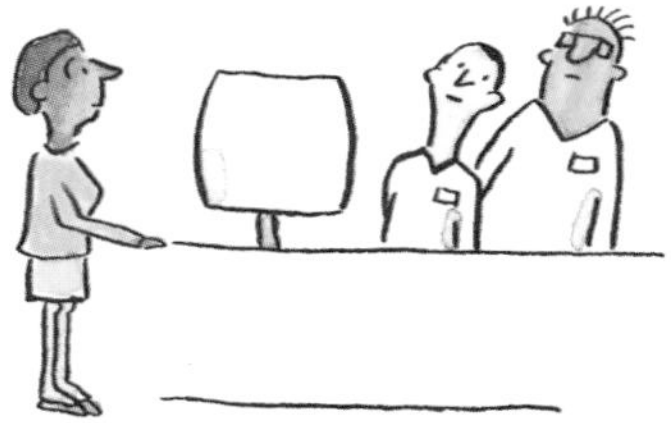

at the Geek Station?

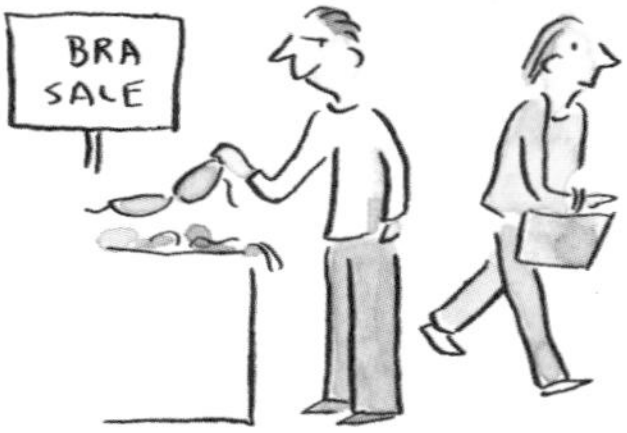
BRA
SALE

at the Mall?

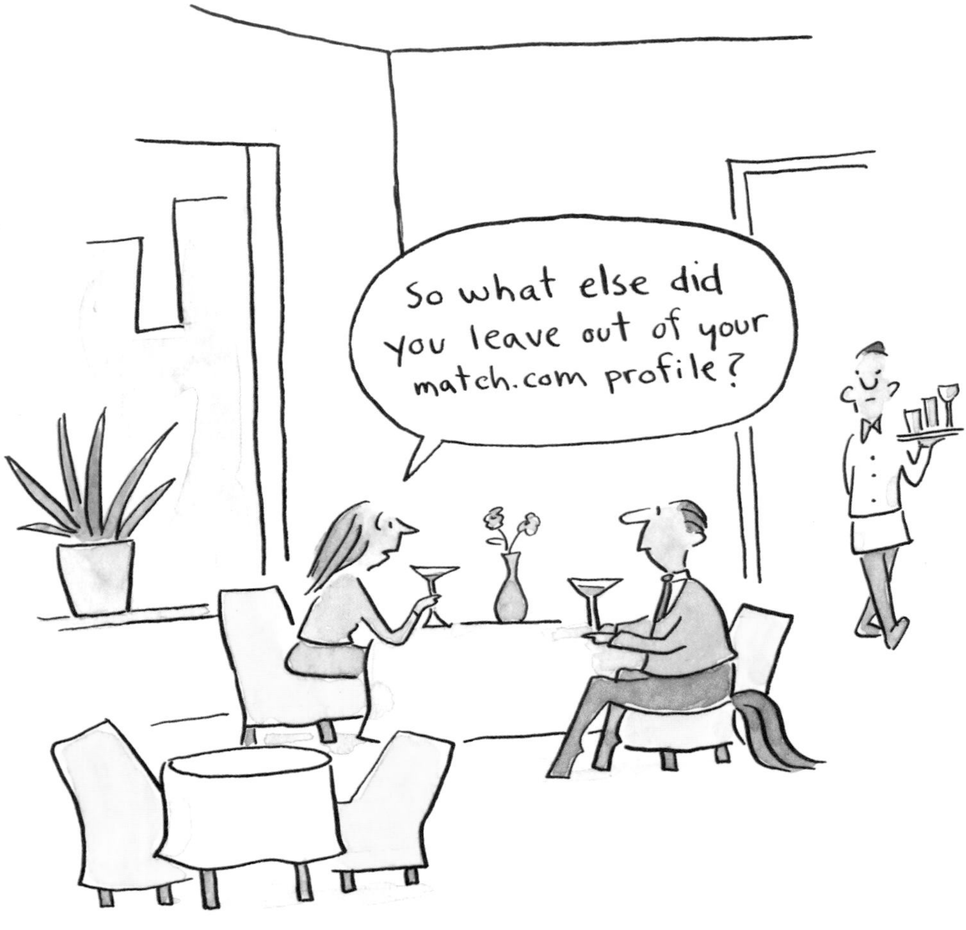
So what else did you leave out of your match.com profile?

Timing

So you've got work figured out—good job, steady pay, room for advancement. You put off settling down for this and it's payed off.

THEN...

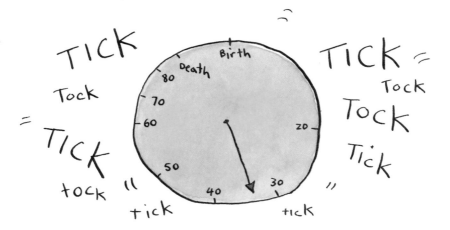

TICK
Tock
= TICK
tock

Birth
80 Death
70
60
50
40
30
20

TICK =
Tock
Tock
Tick

" tick   " tick

The biological clock gets
REALLY LOUD!

Sex in your 30s

Do you let on how much you know?
Do you let on how many?

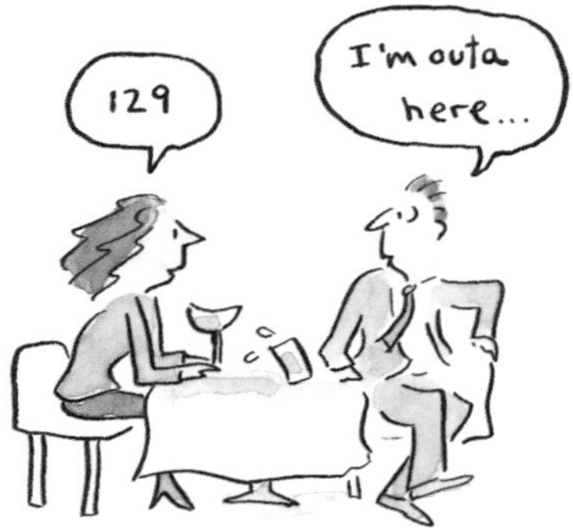
129
I'm outa here...

old-fashioned guy

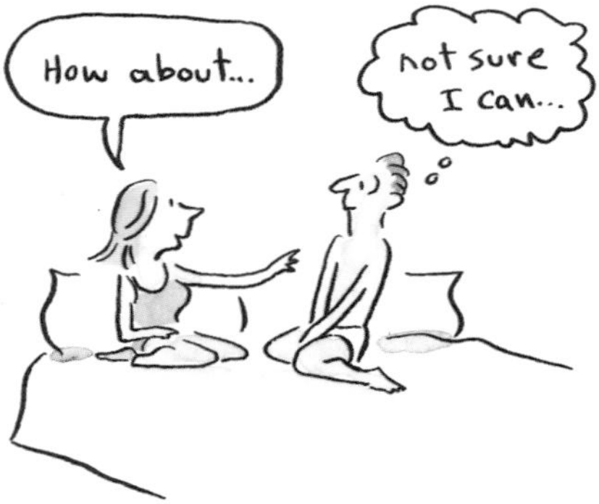
How about...
not sure I can...

insecure guy

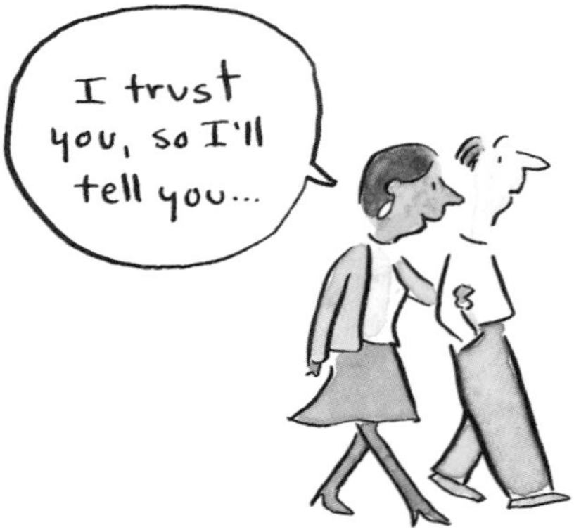
I trust you, so I'll tell you...

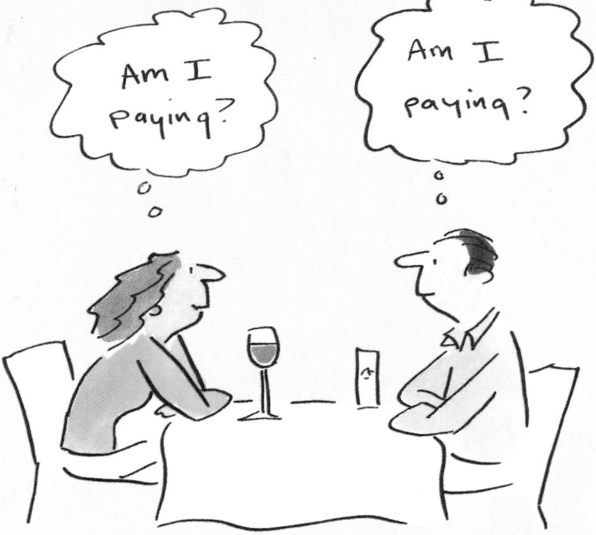
Am I paying?
Am I paying?

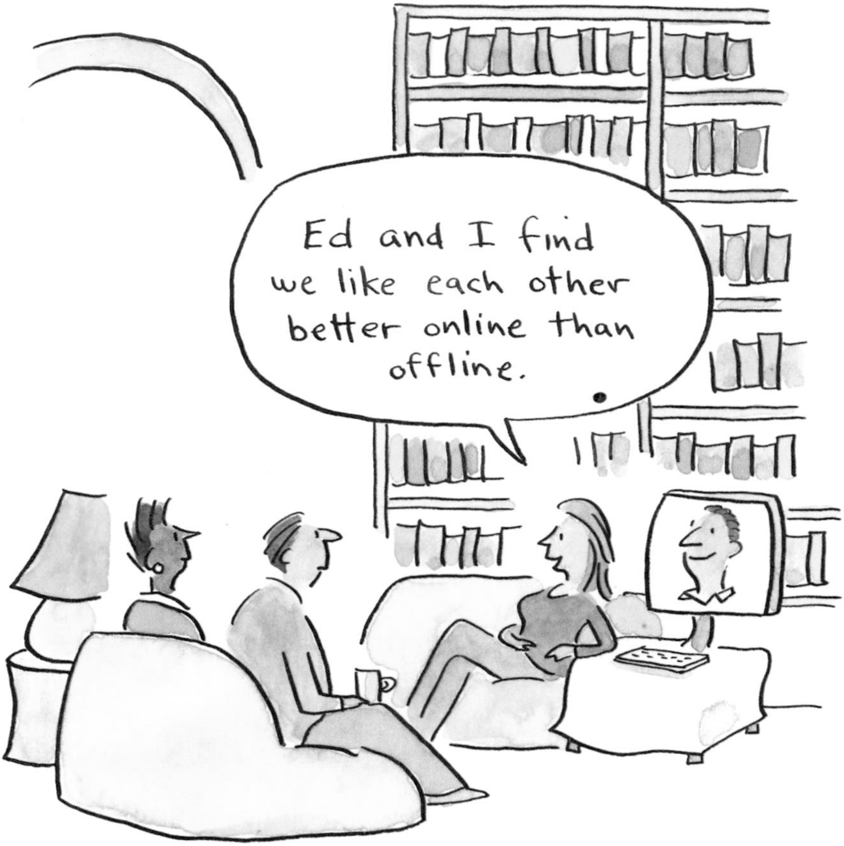
Ed and I find we like each other better online than offline.

Breaking up ~~is hard~~ Gets easier to do

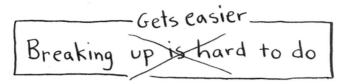

By the time you hit 30, you know when it's not working and don't beat around (excuse the phrase) the bush.

I really like you but I'm not ready.
You're too clingy.
I want to focus on my career.
You are really boring.
It's not you, it's me.
me don't like you.
I hope we can be friends.
sex was really boring with you.
It's not working.
It never worked – should have ended months ago.

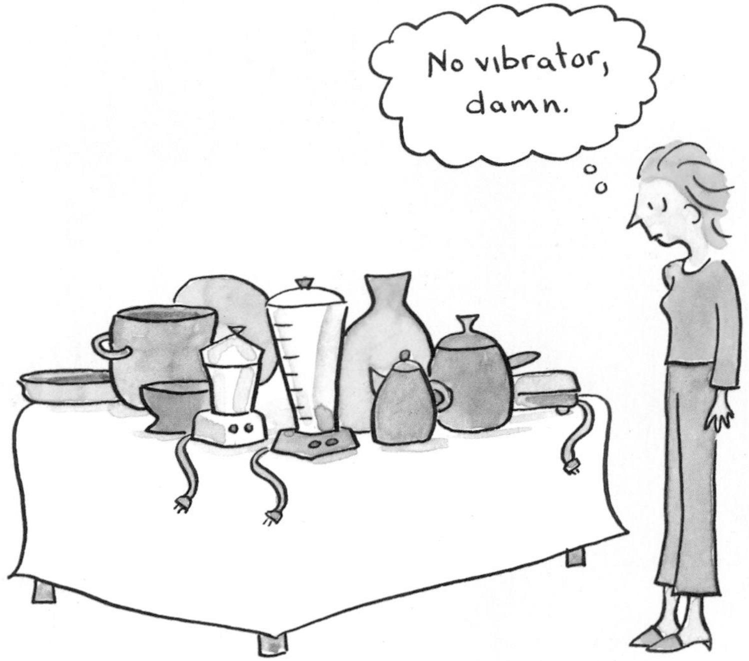
No vibrator, damn.

Shower Gifts

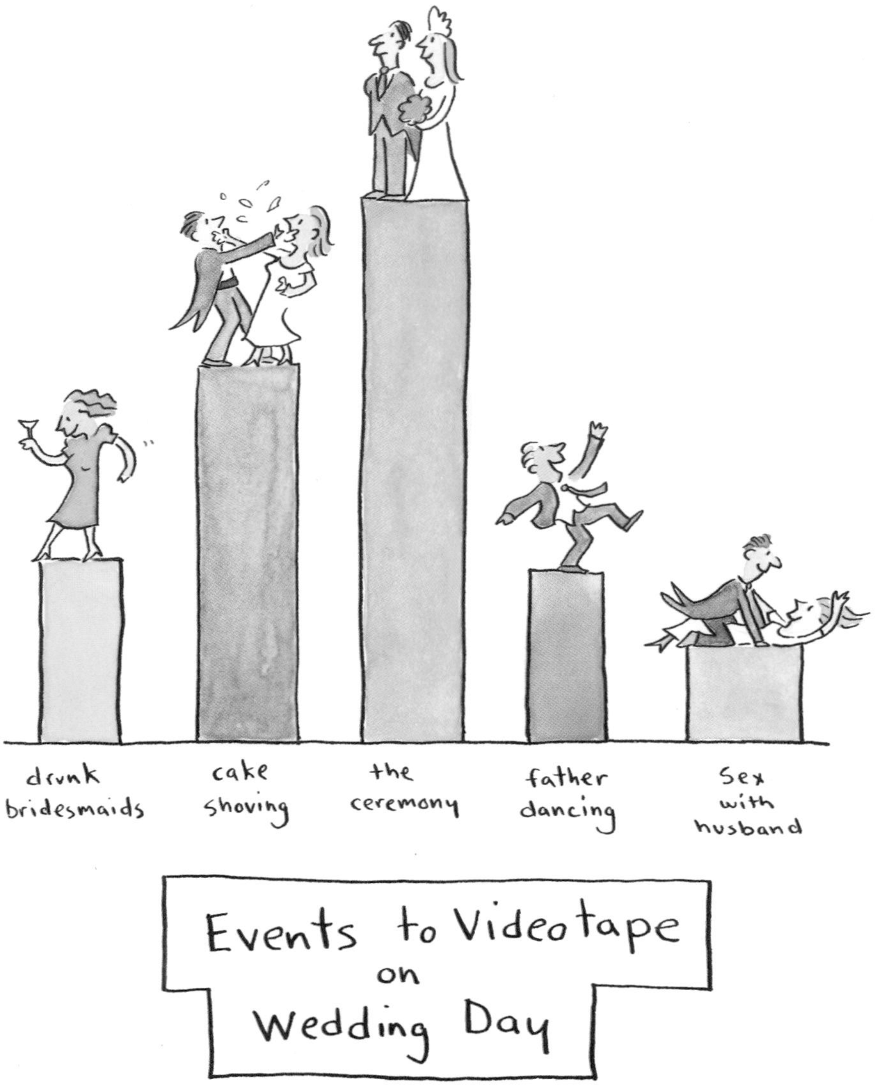
drunk bridesmaids
cake shoving
the ceremony
father dancing
sex with husband
Events to Videotape on Wedding Day

GIRLS NIGHT OUT

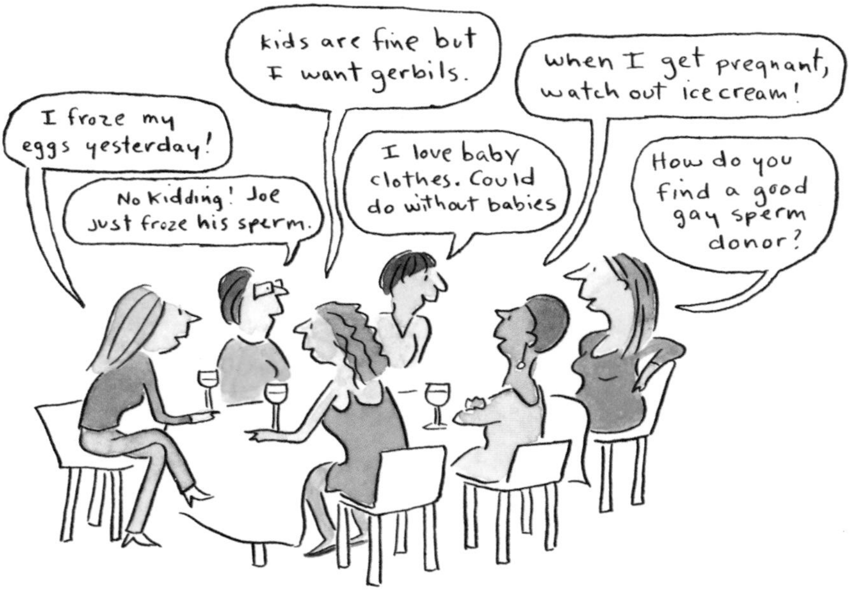
I froze my eggs yesterday!
No Kidding! Joe just froze his sperm.
kids are fine but I want gerbils.
I love baby clothes. Could do without babies
when I get pregnant, watch out ice cream!
How do you find a good gay sperm donor?

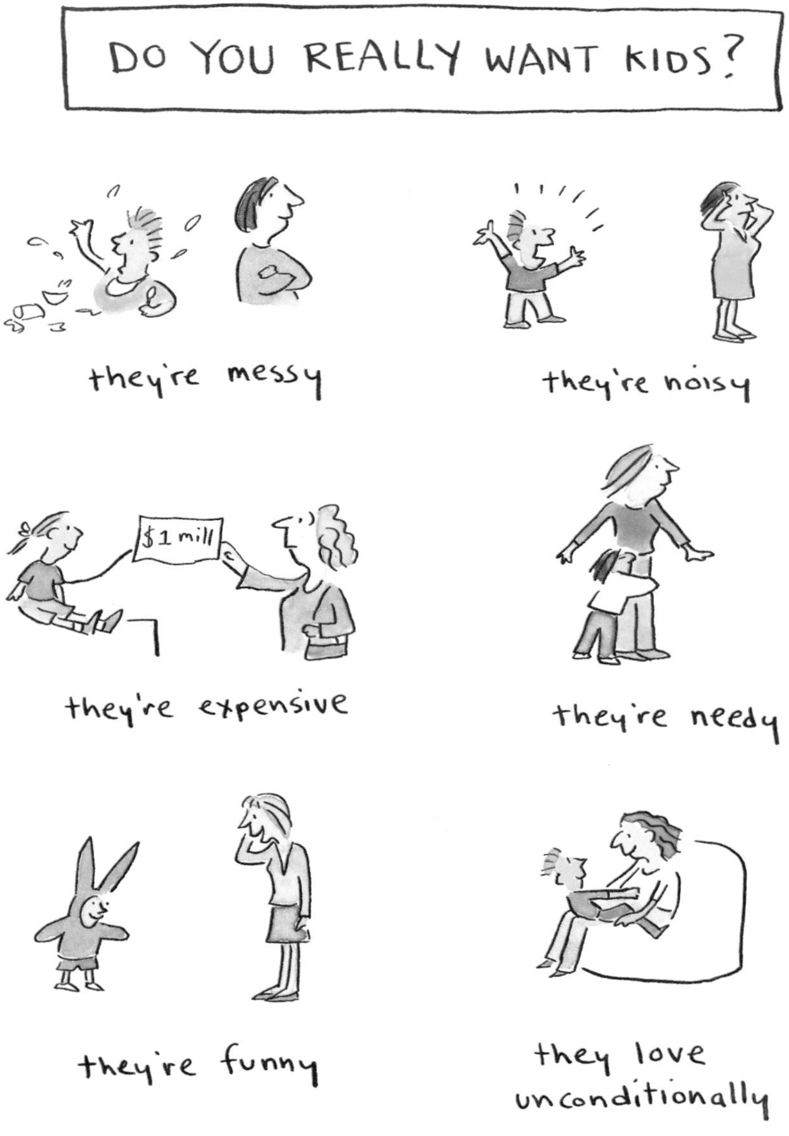
DO YOU REALLY WANT KIDS?
they're messy
they're noisy
$1 mill
they're expensive
they're needy
they're funny
they love unconditionally

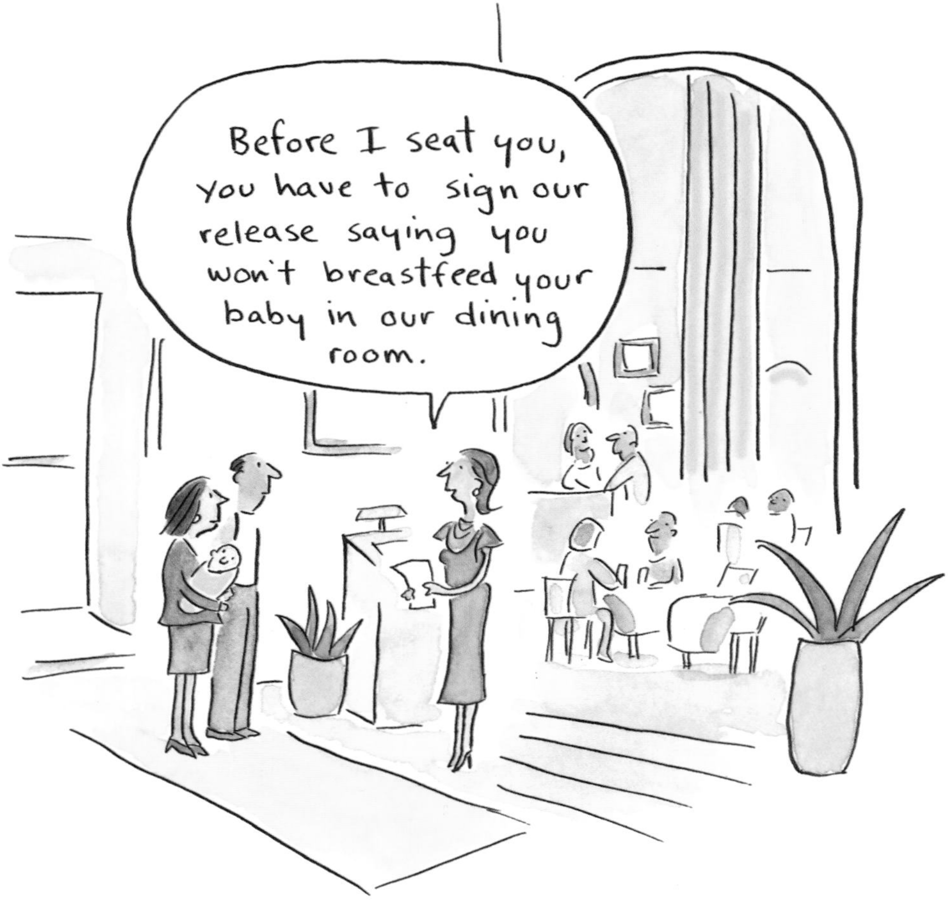
Before I seat you, you have to sign our release saying you won't breastfeed your baby in our dining room.

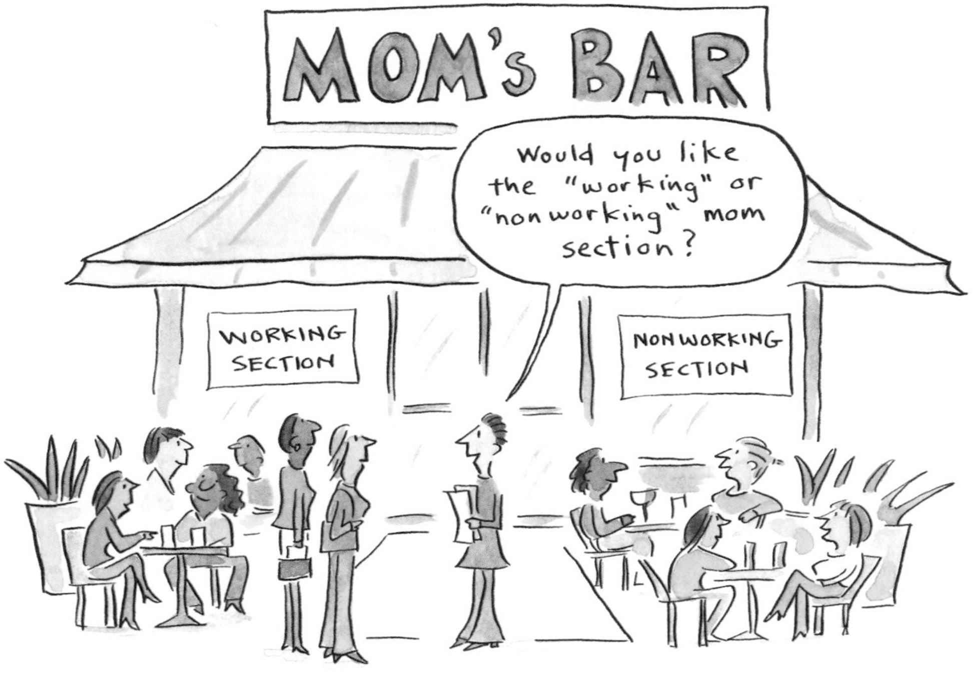
MOM's BAR
Would you like the "working" or "nonworking" mom section?
WORKING SECTION
NONWORKING SECTION

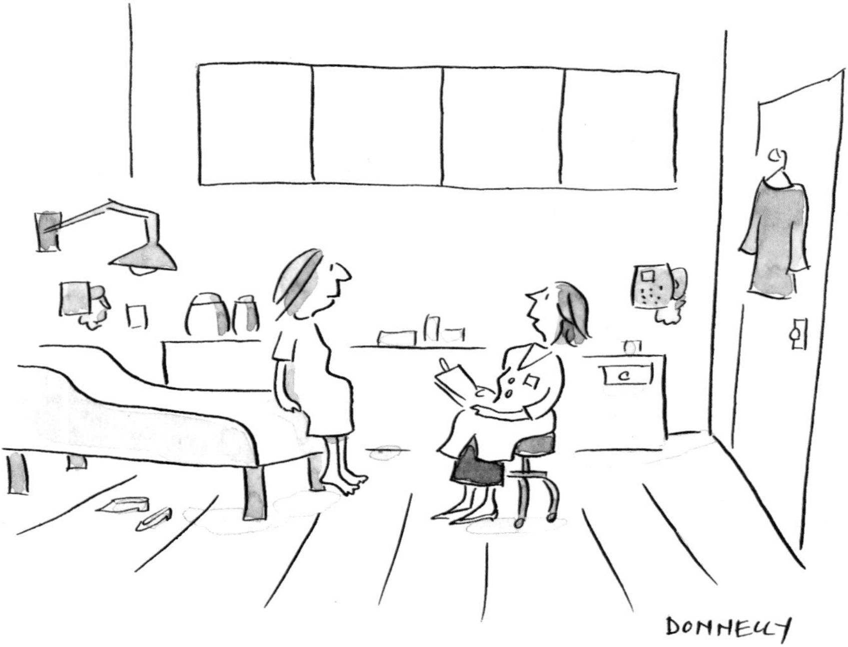
DONNELLY

"Stop looking at women's magazines and call me in the morning."

CHAPTER 4

"What do you do?" This is the pervasive question at parties. But this question takes on a different meaning when you become a mother. As a cartoonist, I could stay home and change diapers while I changed pen nibs. But after childbirth, it is no longer about *you*. It's always about *them*. They own you, your body and mind, for a good 18 years.

I ended up having two beautiful daughters, which, frankly, terrified me. I was told girls are difficult, manipulative, and moody. The mother-daughter complex loomed over me each time the obstetrician said, "It's a girl!"

So what did I do? I baked cupcakes, wiped noses, joined the PTA, and sewed strawberry costumes. Meanwhile, I got a contract at *The New Yorker*, authored seven children's books, wrote a history of the women cartoonists at *The New Yorker,* and compiled three cartoon collections. I even edited a collection of cartoons by women about mothers and daughters to help me understand what the heck I was going through.

Yes, my daughters had tantrums, but they never lived down to the reputation that girls have. They found their way into womanhood with ease, something that I was not so fortunate to experience. I like to think that all my "doing" was of some help.

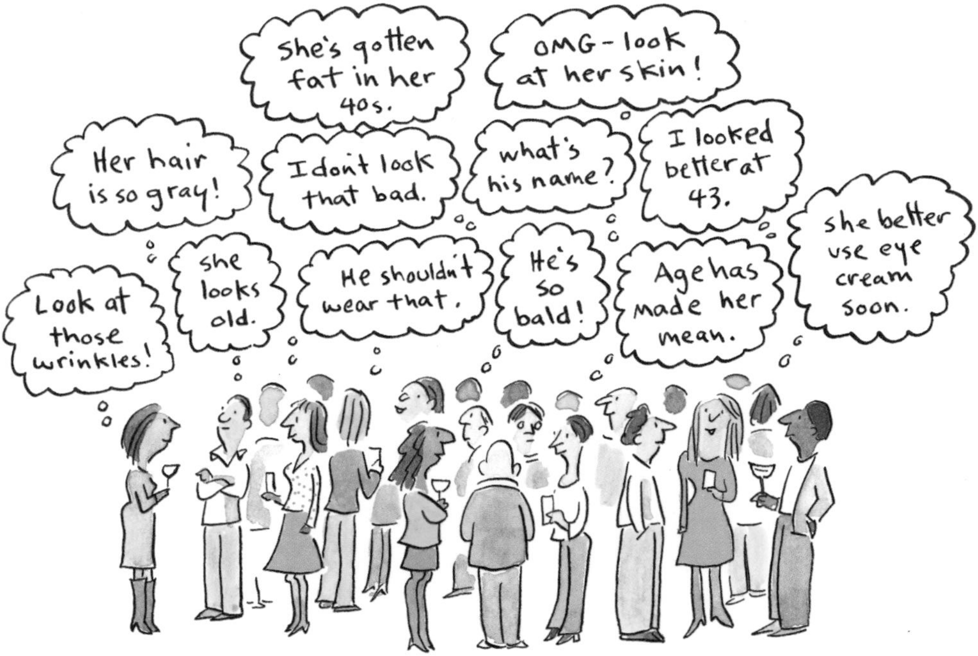
She's gotten fat in her 40s.
OMG-look at her skin!
Her hair is so gray!
I dont look that bad.
what's his name?
I looked better at 43.
she better use eye cream soon.
Look at those wrinkles!
she looks old.
He shouldn't wear that.
He's so bald!
Age has made her mean.

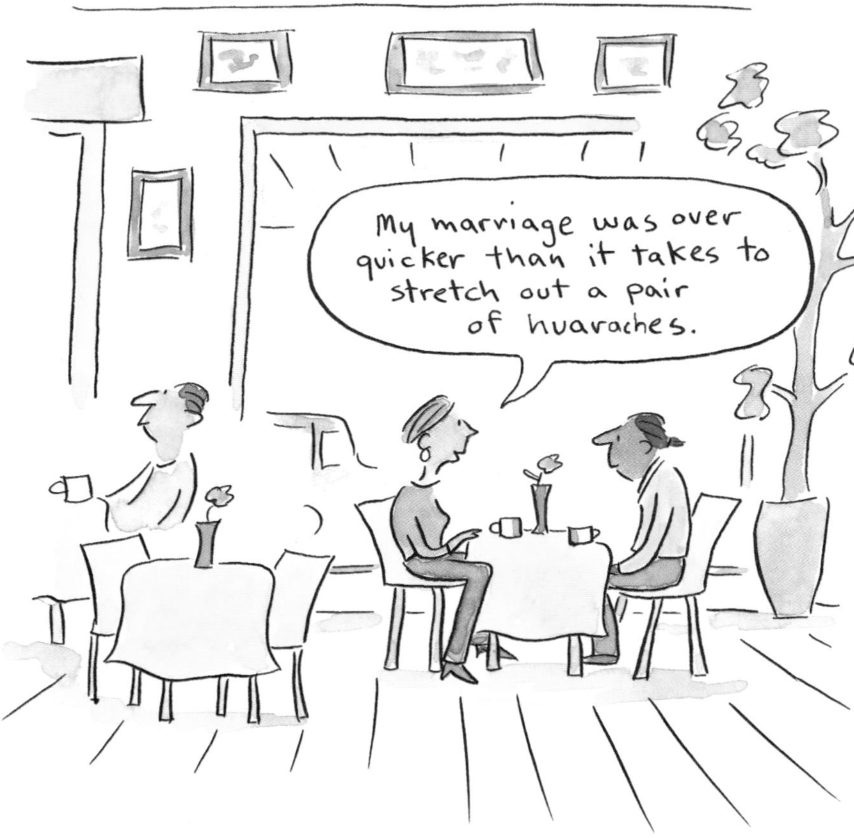
My marriage was over quicker than it takes to stretch out a pair of huaraches.

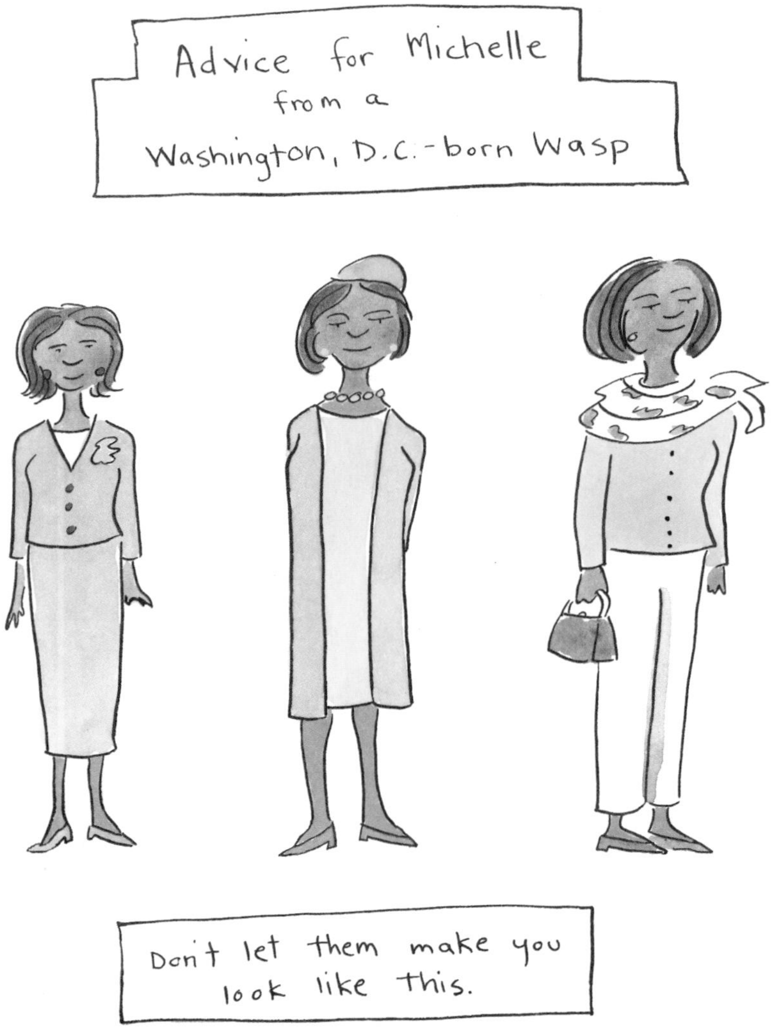
Advice for Michelle
from a
Washington, D.C.-born Wasp
Don't let them make you look like this.

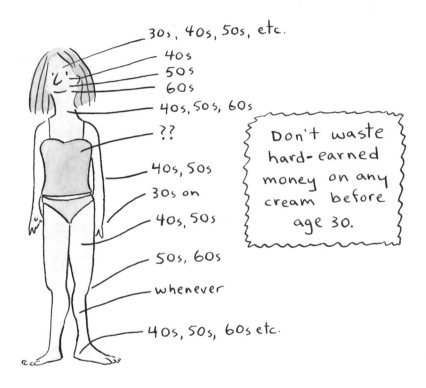

PLACES to PUT CREAM
AND WHEN

30s, 40s, 50s, etc.

40s

50s

60s

40s, 50s, 60s

??

40s, 50s

30s on

40s, 50s

50s, 60s

whenever

40s, 50s, 60s etc.

Don't waste hard-earned money on any cream before age 30.

Cleavage

Why do we bother?

too momish?

my boobs are tiny but I'm desperate for cleavage

high fashion or just really disturbing

show-off to annoy other women

If you look like this in your 40s, people will assume...

- You are a mother
- You aren't "getting any"
- You spent ten years on a commune in the '60s
- You abhor women's magazines

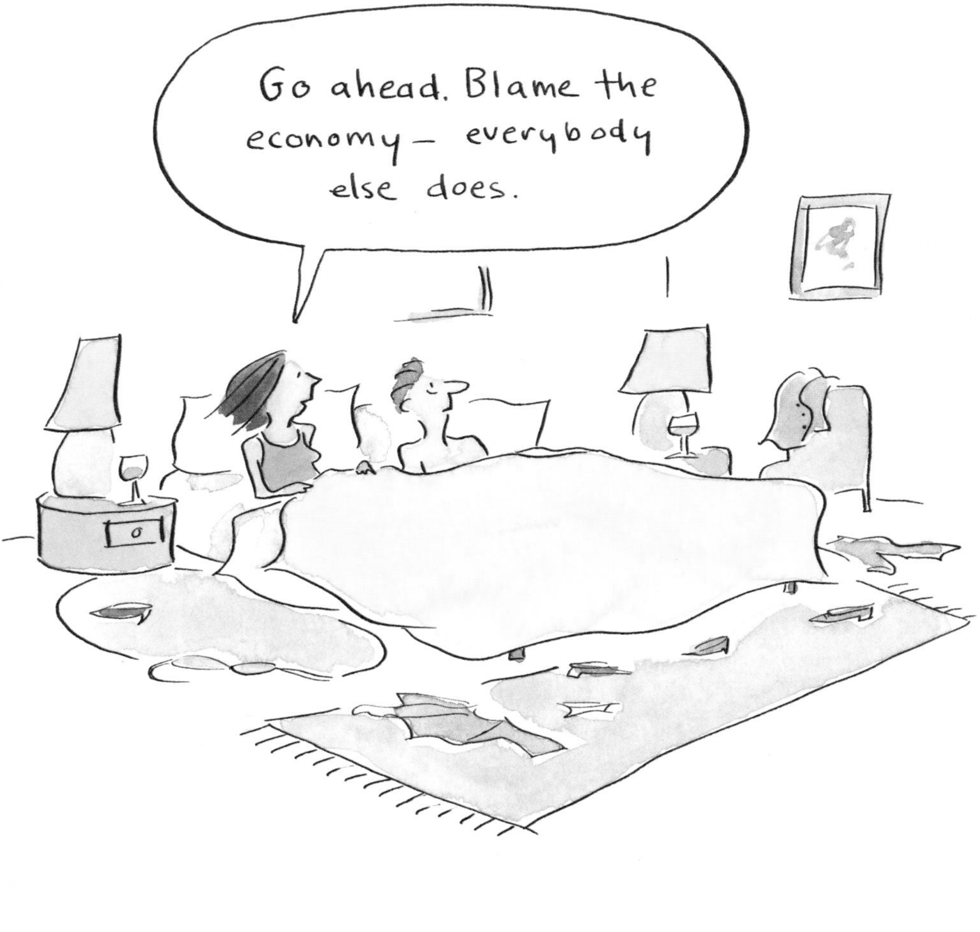
Go ahead. Blame the economy– everybody else does.

HAIRSTYLES to AVOID in your 40s

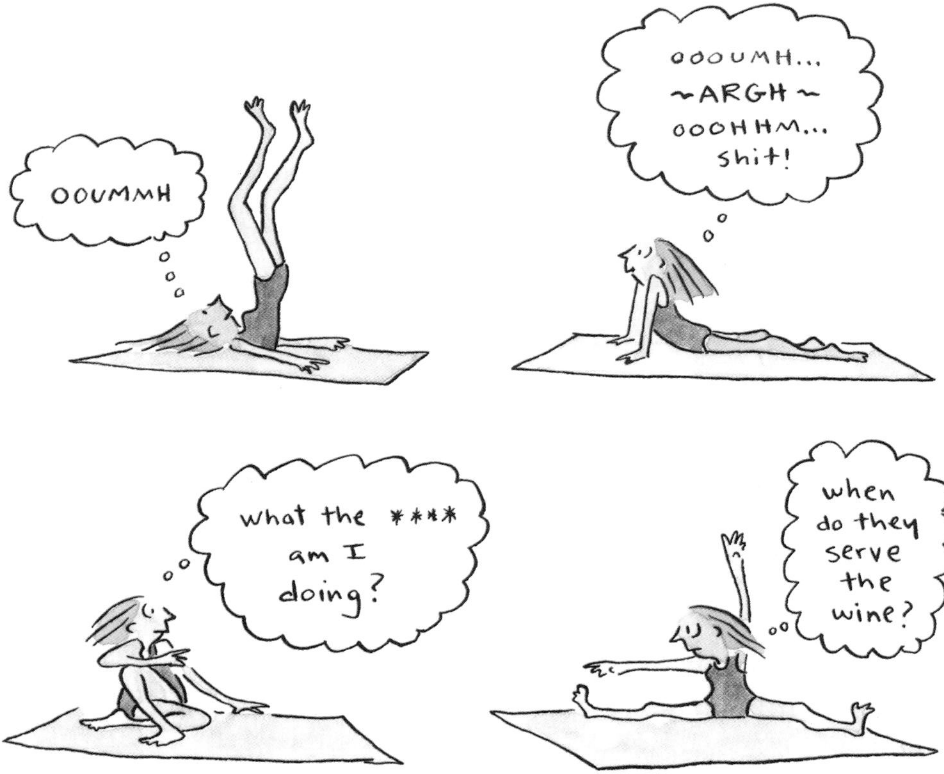
OOUMMH
OOOUMH...
~ARGH~
OOOHHM...
shit!
what the **** am I doing?
when do they serve the wine?

You ask your Hair Stylist for something "New + Age Appropriate"

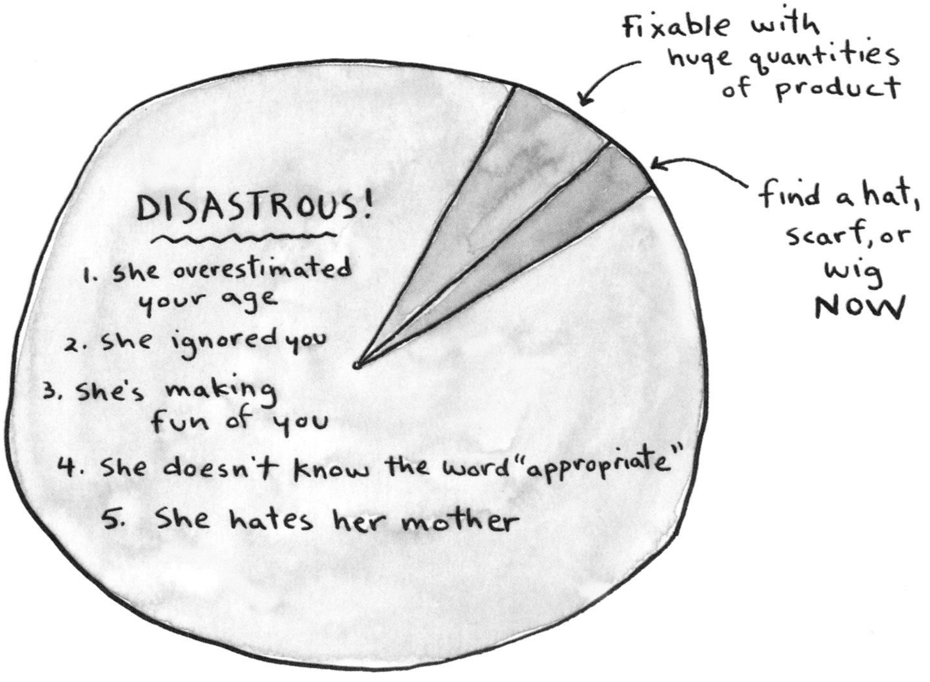
Fixable with huge quantities of product
find a hat, scarf, or wig NOW
DISASTROUS!
1. She overestimated your age
2. She ignored you
3. She's making fun of you
4. She doesn't know the word "appropriate"
5. She hates her mother

Which Body Shape are You?

pear

apple

banana

ice cream cone

GIRLS NIGHT OUT

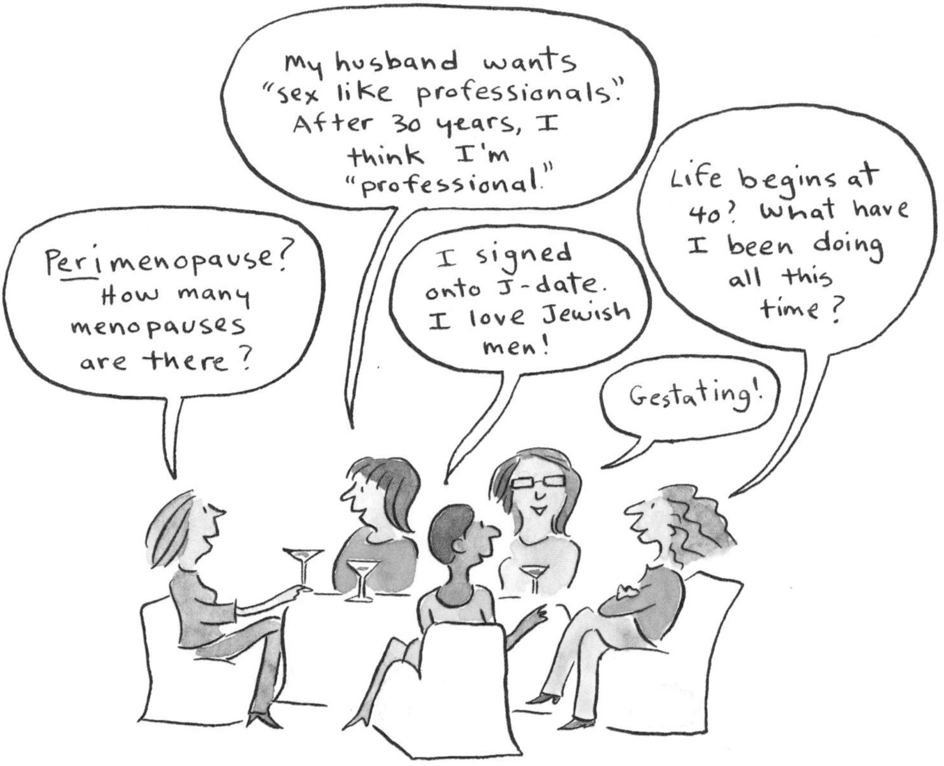
Perimenopause? How many menopauses are there?
My husband wants "sex like professionals." After 30 years, I think I'm "professional."
I signed onto J-date. I love Jewish men!
Life begins at 40? What have I been doing all this time?
Gestating!

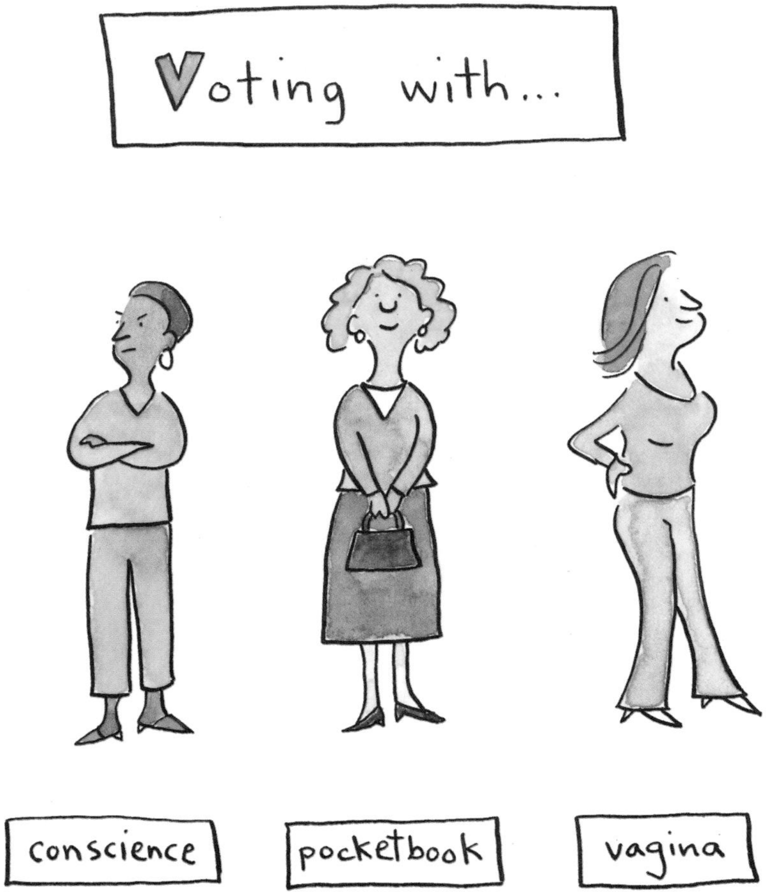
Voting with...
conscience
pocketbook
vagina

How to tell if he's cheating

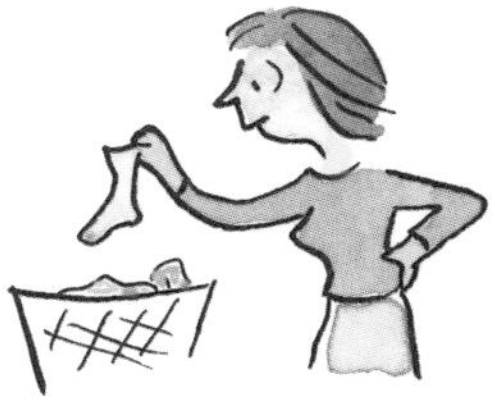

Lipstick on his socks (and shirt and tie and pants and...)

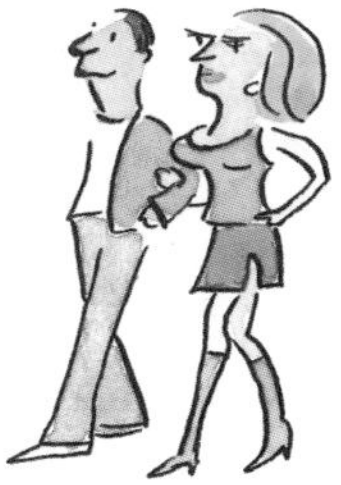

He's spotted with...

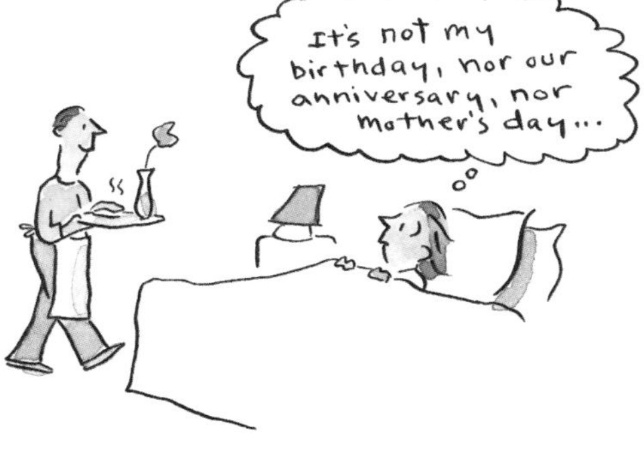
It's not my birthday, nor our anniversary, nor mother's day...

He's extraordinarily helpful.

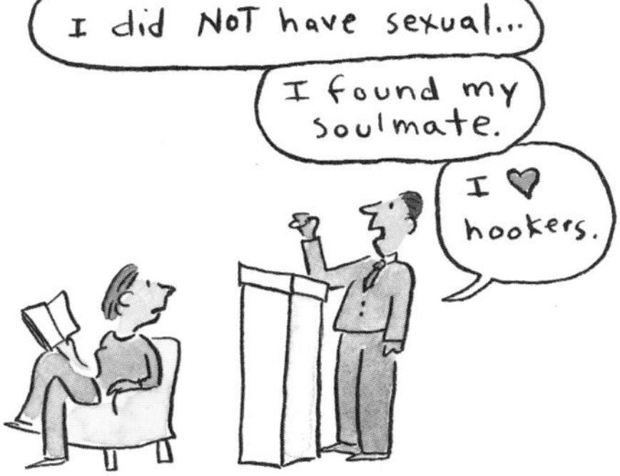
I did NOT have sexual...
I found my soulmate.
I ♥ hookers.

Does he act like Clinton, Spitzer, or Sanford?

To help prepare the suit, I'll need to ask you a number of questions about your former husband, hereafter called "son-of-a-bitch."

You know your Sex Life is doomed when

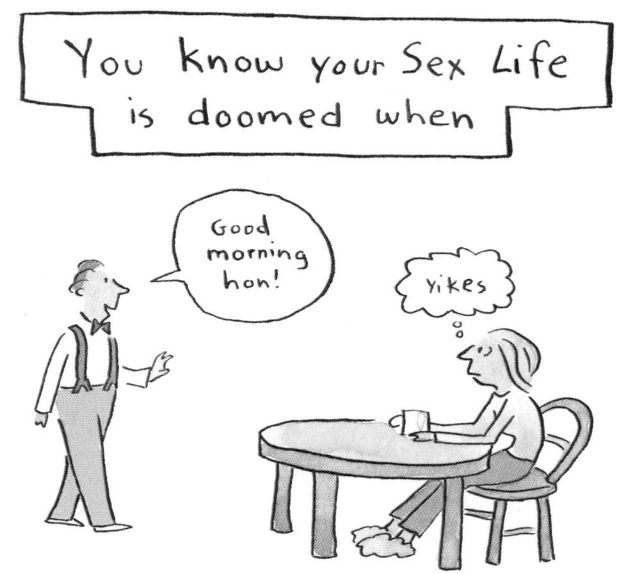
Good morning hon!
yikes

He starts happily wearing bow ties and suspenders.

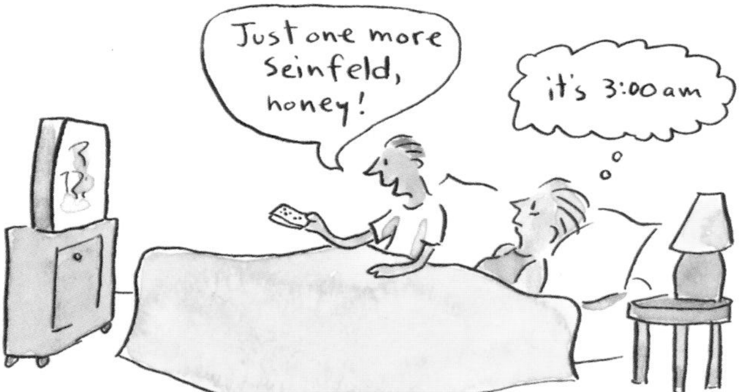
Just one more Seinfeld, honey!
it's 3:00 am

Comedy becomes more fun.

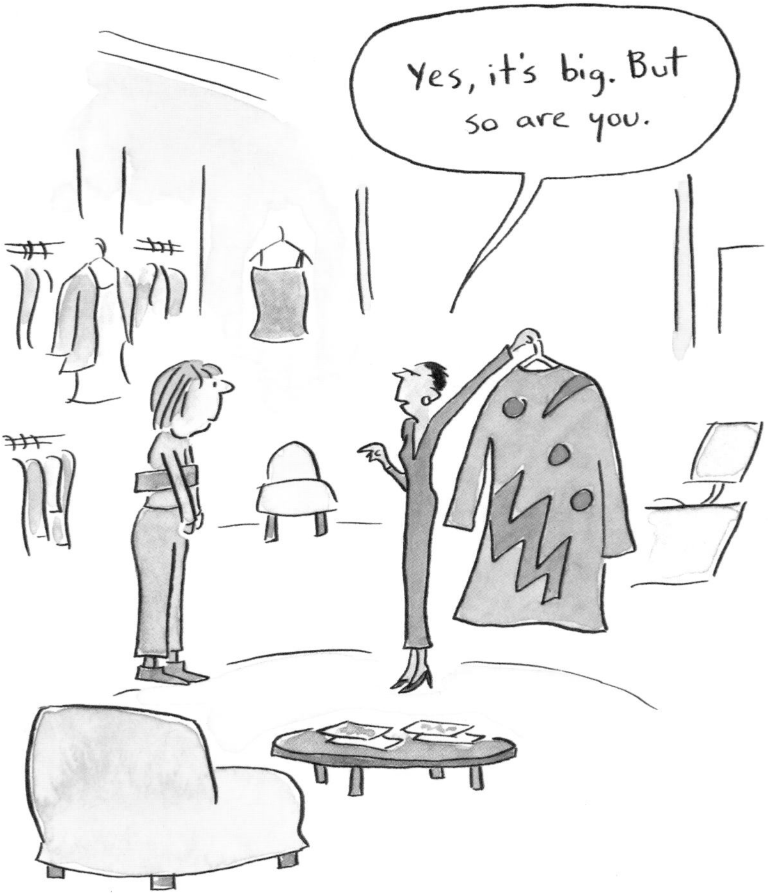
Yes, it's big. But so are you.

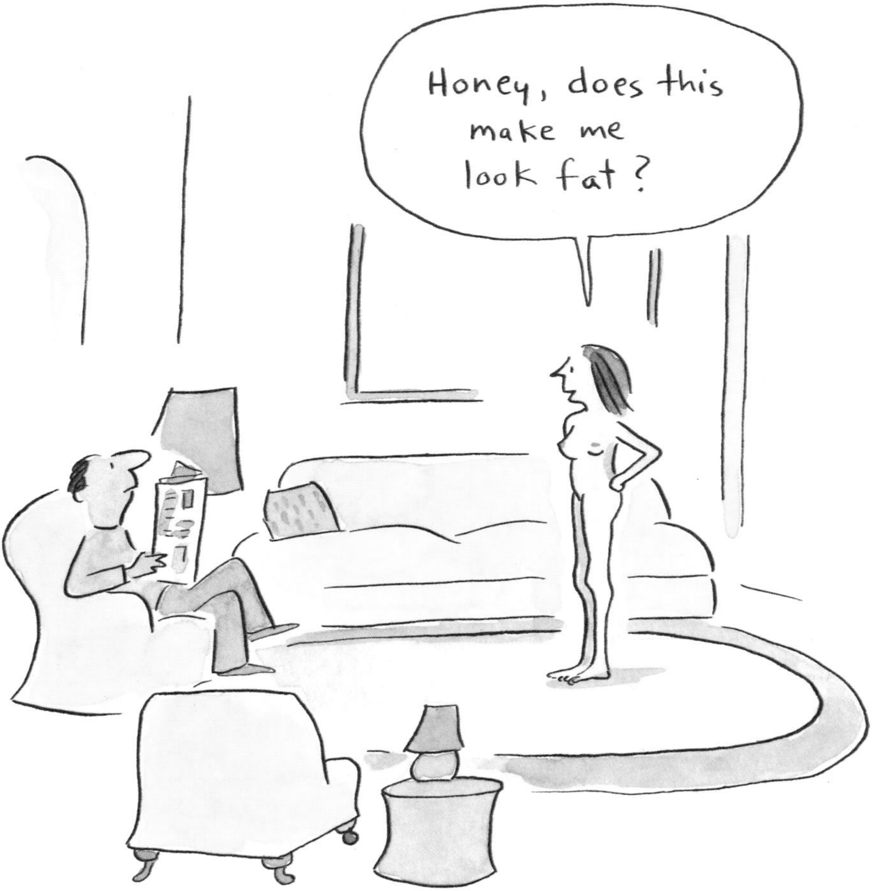
Honey, does this make me look fat?

I dreamt I was being cornered by giant wrinkles and tortured by menopause until a handsome plastic surgeon came and rescued me. What does it mean?

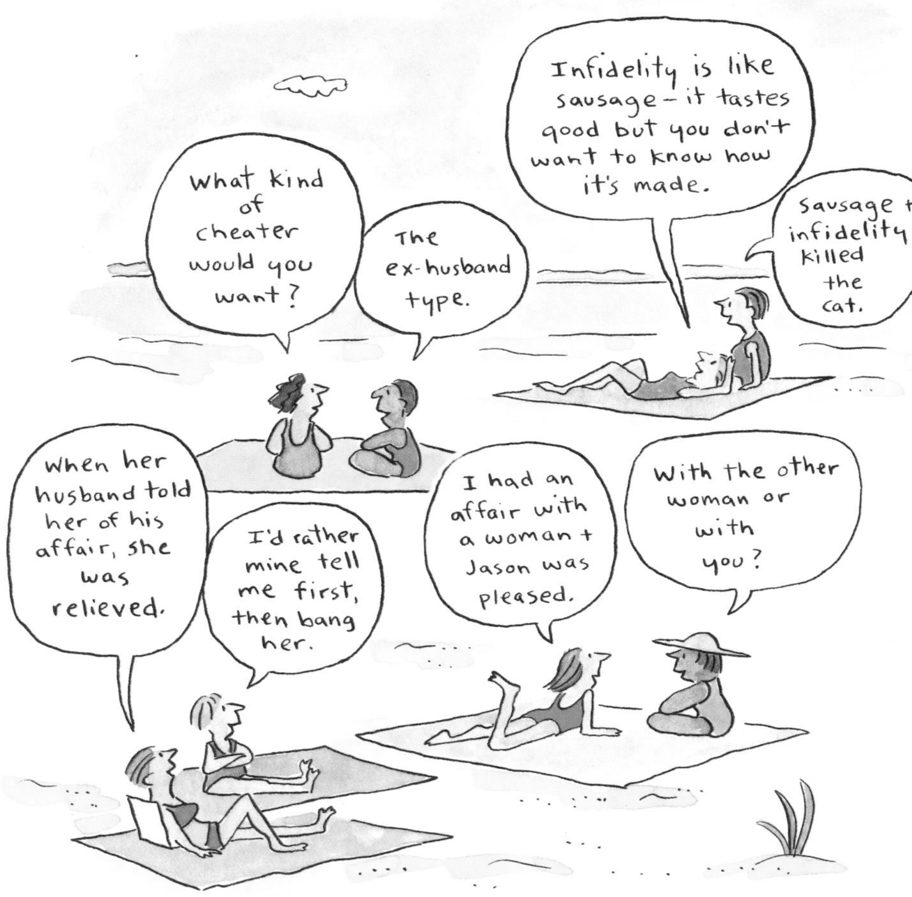
What kind of cheater would you want?
The ex-husband type.
Infidelity is like sausage – it tastes good but you don't want to know how it's made.
Sausage + infidelity killed the cat.
When her husband told her of his affair, she was relieved.
I'd rather mine tell me first, then bang her.
I had an affair with a woman + Jason was pleased.
With the other woman or with you?

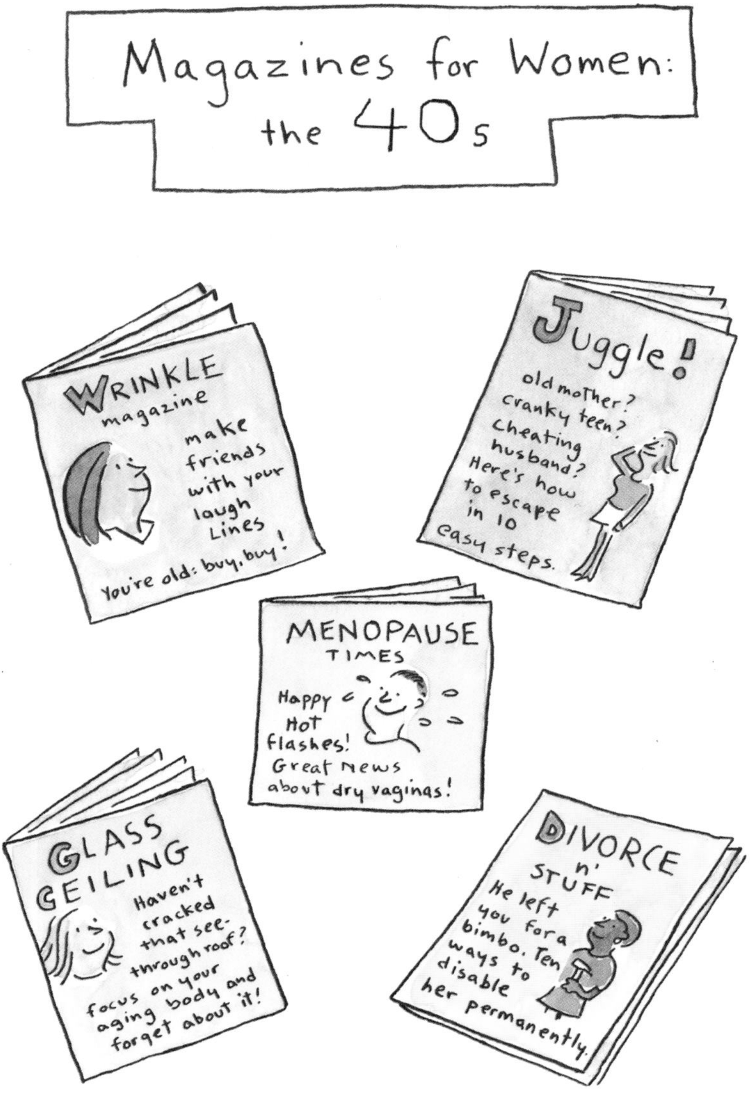
Magazines for Women: the 40s
WRINKLE magazine
make friends with your laugh Lines
You're old: buy, buy!
Juggle!
old mother? cranky teen? Cheating husband? Here's how to escape in 10 easy steps.
MENOPAUSE TIMES
Happy Hot flashes!
Great News about dry vaginas!
GLASS CEILING
Haven't cracked that see-through roof?
focus on your aging body and forget about it!
DIVORCE n' STUFF
He left you for a bimbo. Ten ways to disable her permanently.

Noncommittal Men

He won't commit to any number of domestic chores because he agreed to the big committment: marriage.

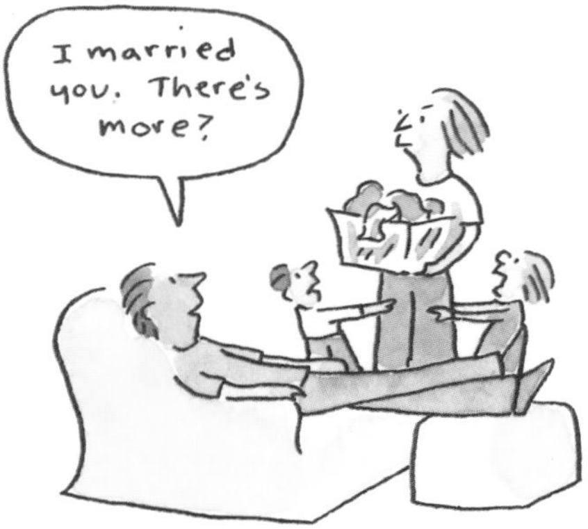
I married you. There's more?

~ OR ~

He won't commit to chilling about your larger paycheck.

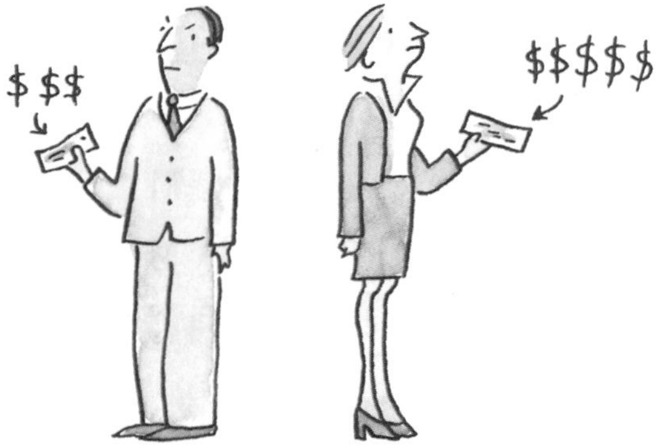
$$$
$$$$$

LIPOSUCTION and YOU

Before you go under the vacuum, consider:

1. diet and exercise.

2. not looking so closely.

3. getting yelled at by loved ones who don't want you to do it.

Death from unnecessary surgery

4. Get a reality check.

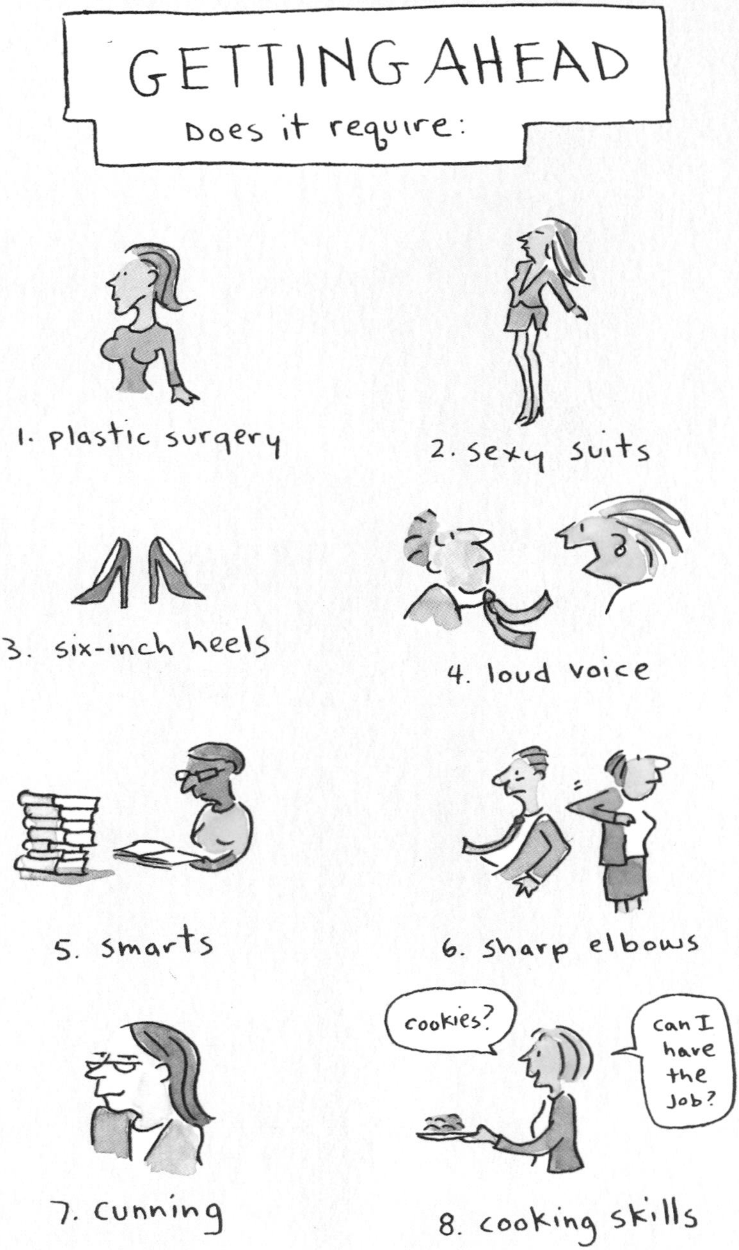
GETTING AHEAD
Does it require:
1. plastic surgery
2. sexy suits
3. six-inch heels
4. loud voice
5. smarts
6. sharp elbows
cookies?
Can I have the Job?
7. cunning
8. cooking skills

GRAY HAIR

Many women never color their hair, so ease into, without confusion, being gray.

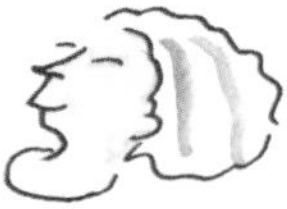

Some are lucky to have hair that grays interestingly.

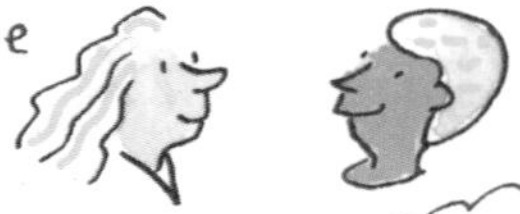

But some women have NO IDEA what color their hair actually is, they've been coloring it for 30 years.

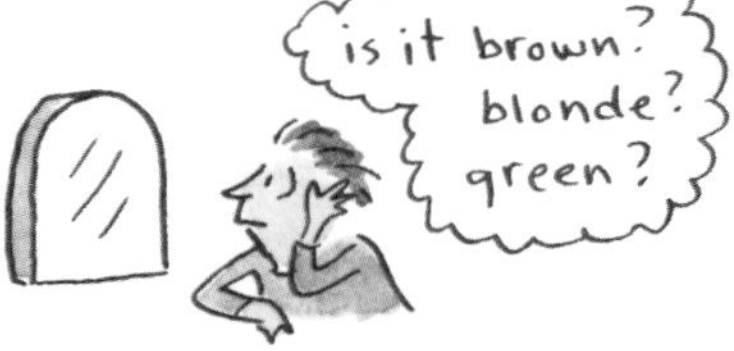
is it brown? blonde? green?

THE QUESTIONS ARE:

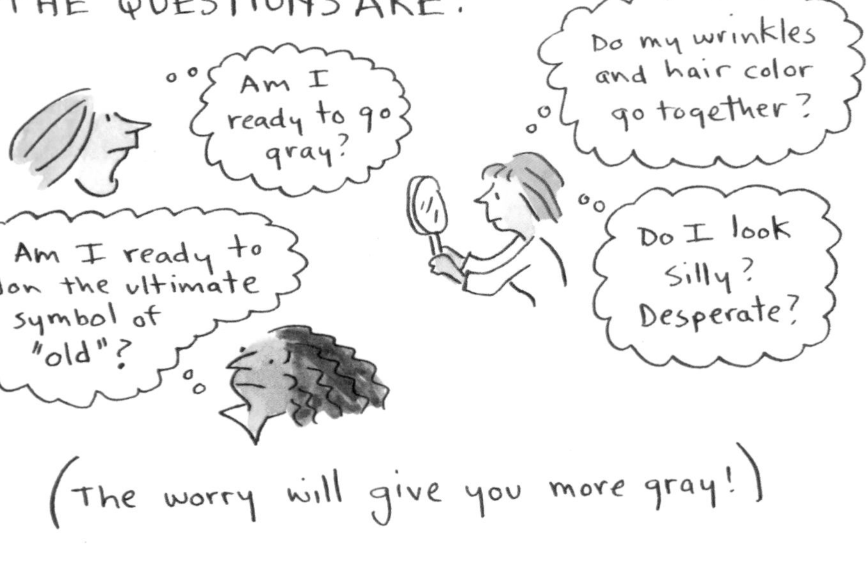
Am I ready to go gray?
Do my wrinkles and hair color go together?
Do I look Silly? Desperate?
Am I ready to don the ultimate symbol of "old"?

(The worry will give you more gray!)

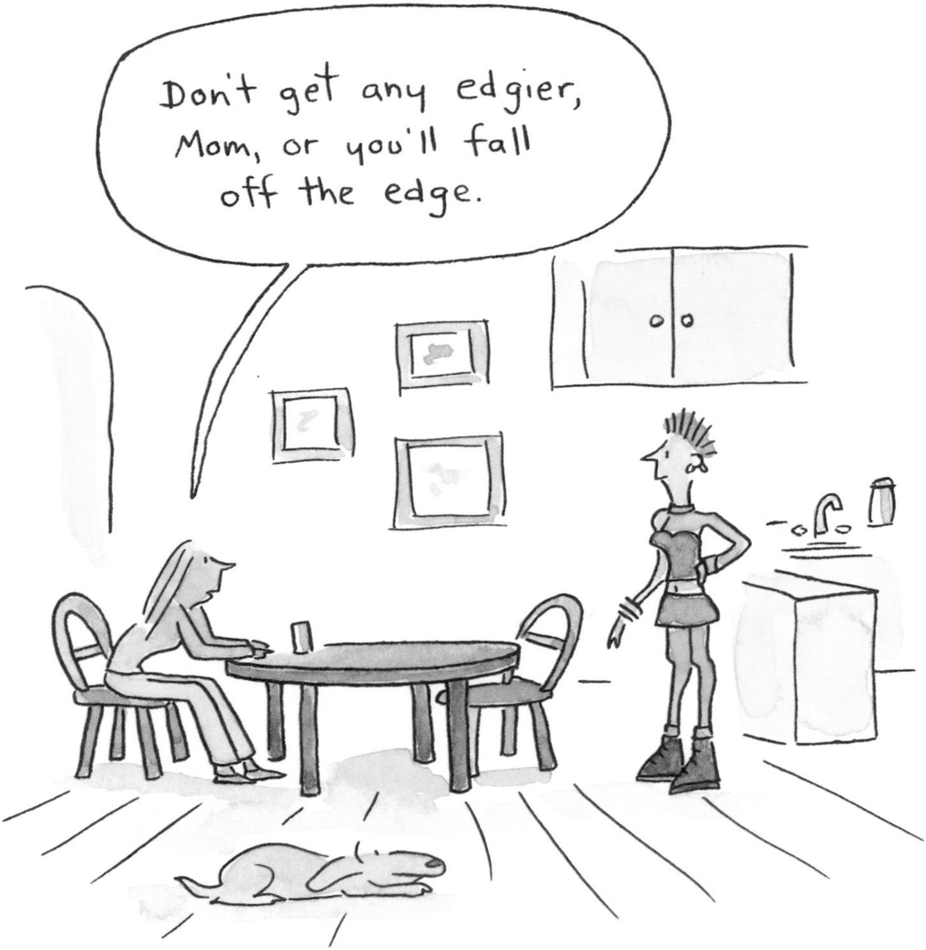
Don't get any edgier, Mom, or you'll fall off the edge.

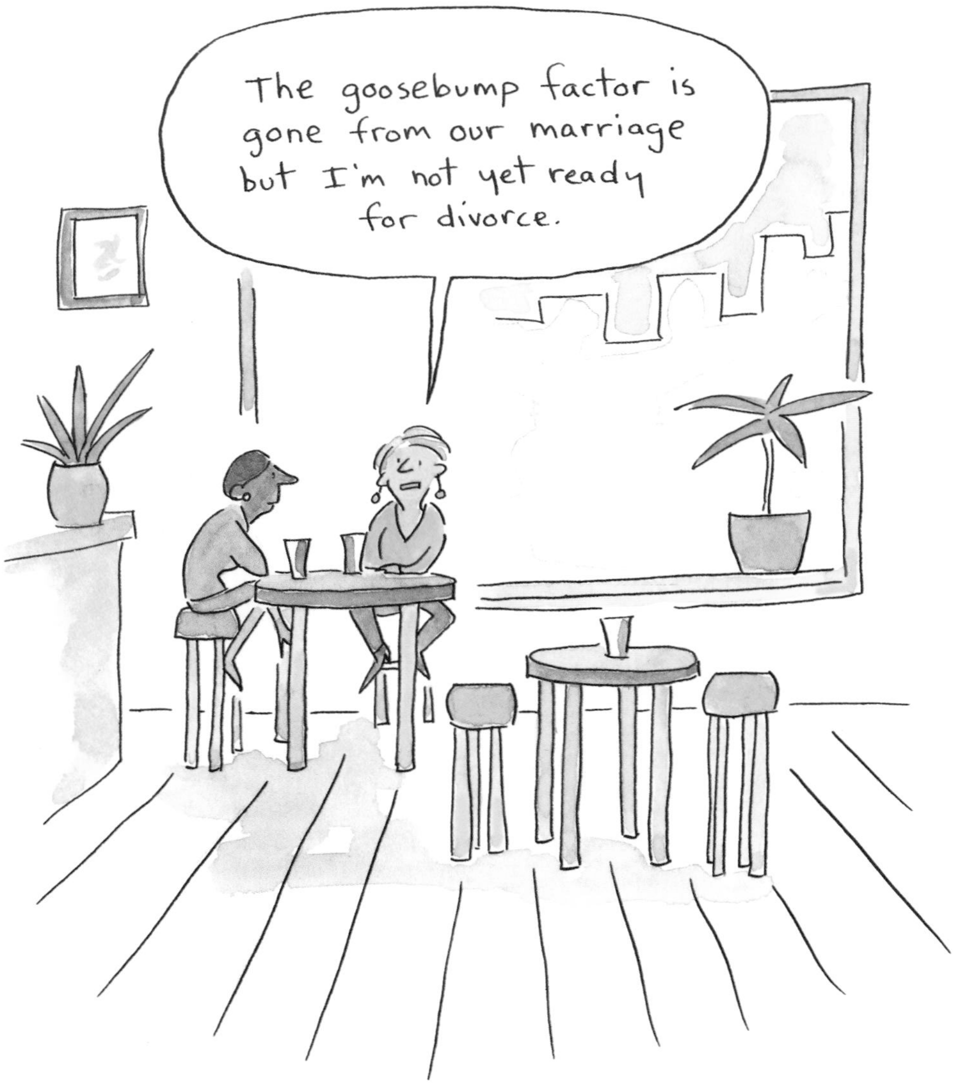
The goosebump factor is gone from our marriage but I'm not yet ready for divorce.

Advances for Women

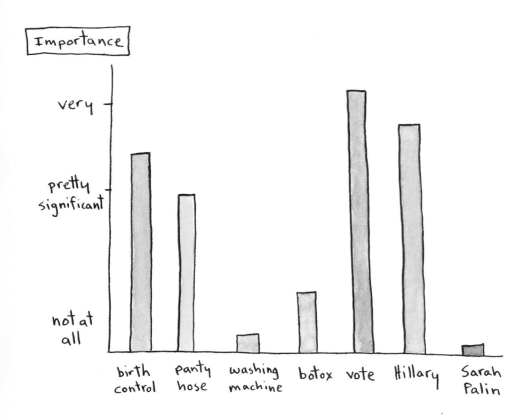

Importance

very —

pretty
significant —

not at
all

birth control · panty hose · washing machine · botox · vote · Hillary · Sarah Palin

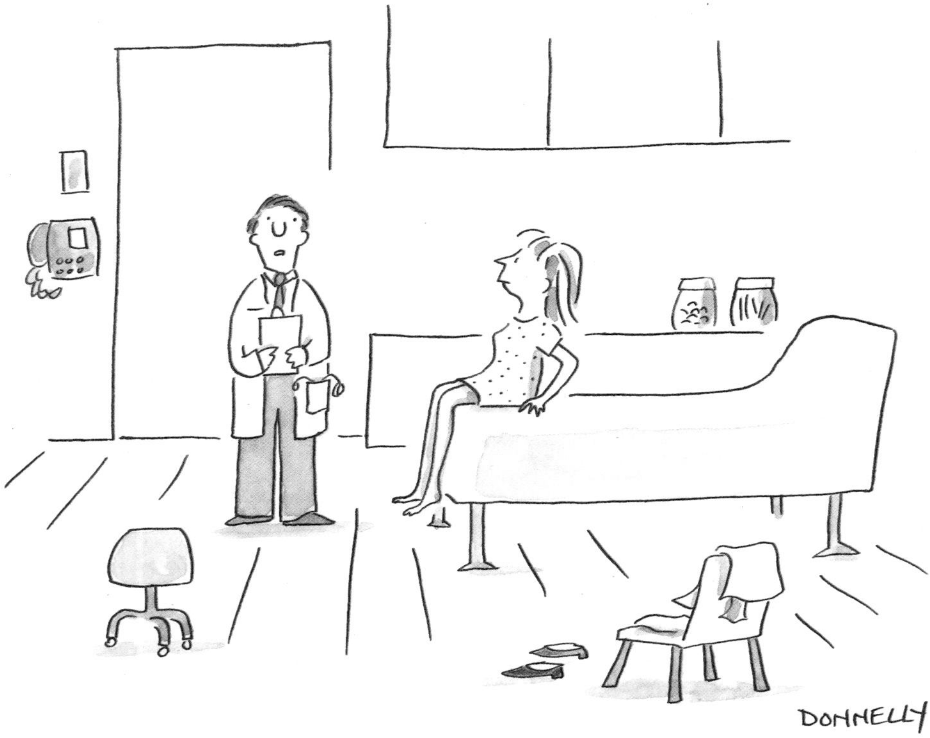
DONNELLY

"If I tell you your problem is old age, will you sue me?"

CHAPTER 5

50s

I always prided myself on the fact that I didn't buy a lot of face "product"—just soap. Then I turned 50. Strange little lines started to appear on my face. What *are* those? *Wrinkles*? I finally peered at the stuff in the cosmetic aisles at the drugstore—the area that looks vaguely like a doctor's office. I felt self-conscious. There were pots of things with names like: rejuvionolum method for early nighttime under-eye brightening and lifting, serumtology-inspired management system for total lip care, exfoliating system essentials for neck management during lunchtime. I purchased a $15, 1.5-ounce tube of eye cream and escaped unnoticed.

I spent a good part of my youth aware that I was being looked at—as a woman, and especially for my long blonde hair. I dressed for others: women, men, my grandmother, my editor, my deli owner—you name it. But in my 50s, I found myself in a new phase of always going unnoticed (except by my husband). This was something of a relief. Yet while this made me angry, it made me want to conform. And buy those $15 tiny tubes.

Maybe this was a small silver lining of going unnoticed—I could be content with how I looked because it wasn't really about what it used to be about. Now it was about what *I* wanted it to be about. Heck, no one will notice anyway.

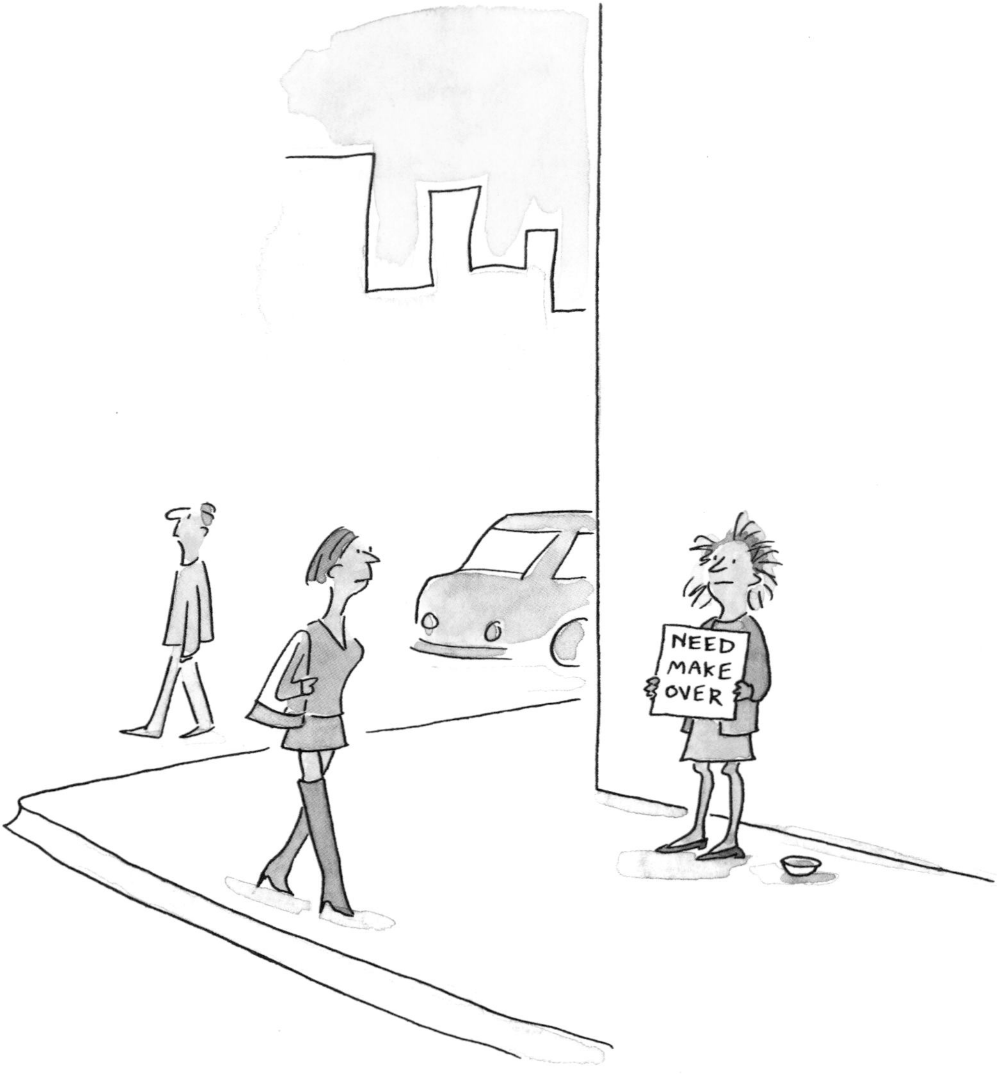
NEED
MAKE
OVER

You know you're getting older when

You think annual negative pap smear results are thrilling.

You don't care how cold the gynecological stirrups are.

You regularly and willingly submit to the smashing of your breasts in a machine.

You talk to complete strangers about hot flashes.

Things to Avoid when over 50

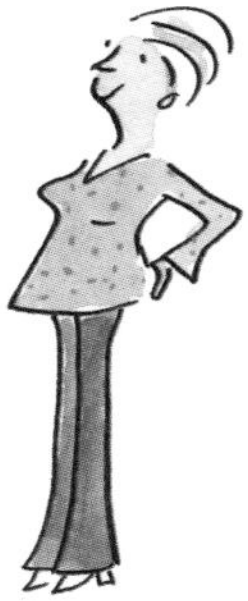

too much purple

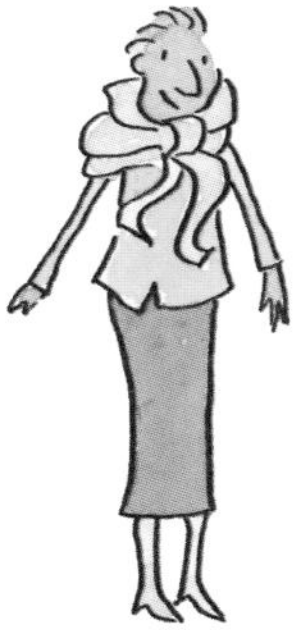

too much scarf

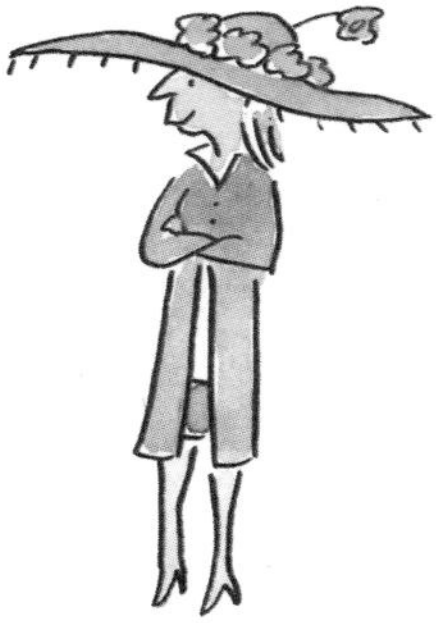

too much hat

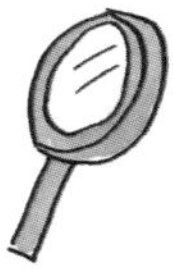

mirrors

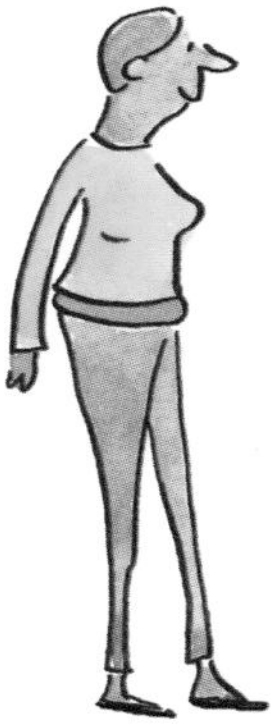

low-rise, skinny jeans

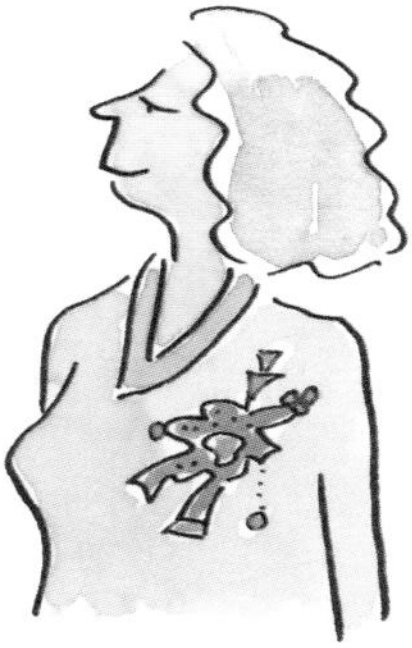

brooches

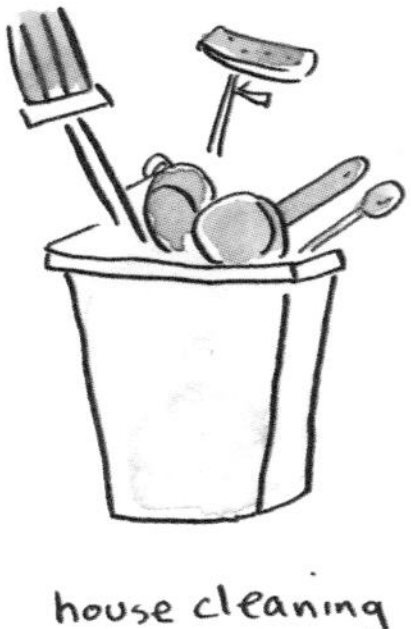

house cleaning and cooking (havent you done enough?)

If you look like this in your 50s, people will assume...

- You are an ambitious bitch.

- You never had children.

- You pussy-whip your husband.

- You are a closet lesbian.

- You slept your way to your position to afford the expensive suit.

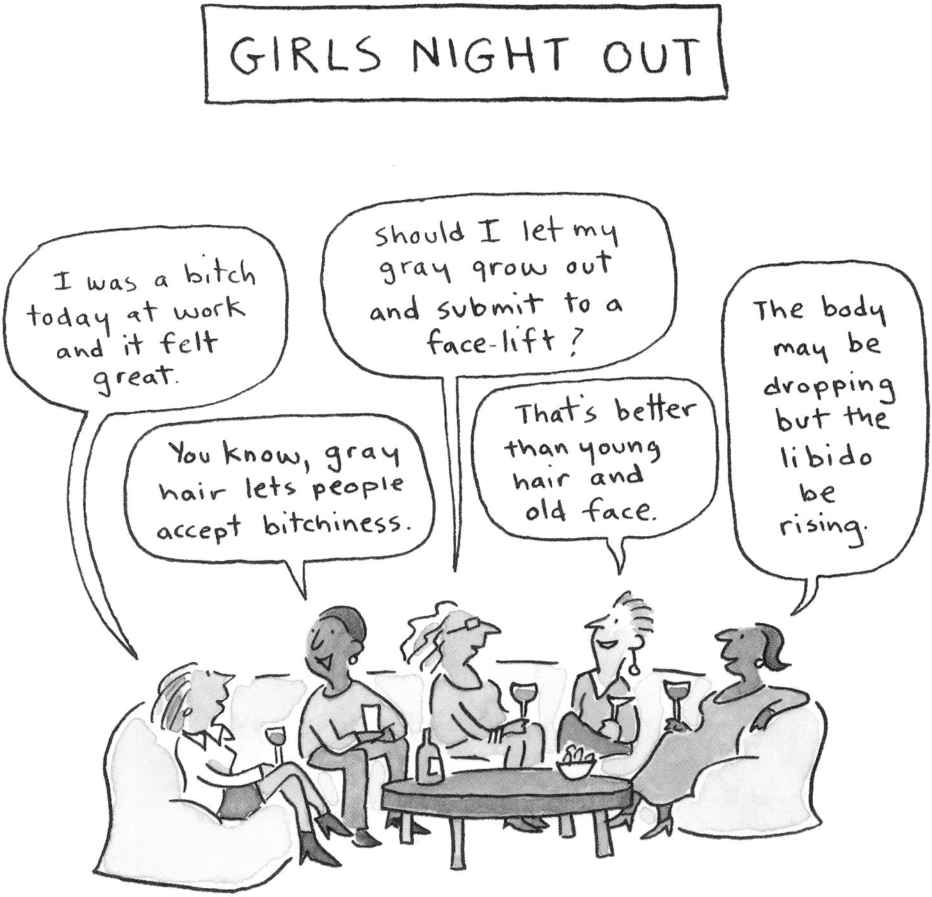
GIRLS NIGHT OUT
I was a bitch today at work and it felt great.
You know, gray hair lets people accept bitchiness.
Should I let my gray grow out and submit to a face-lift?
That's better than young hair and old face.
The body may be dropping but the libido be rising.

HAIRSTYLES to AVOID
in your 50s

Reading glasses

(men do make passes at
girls who wear glasses.)

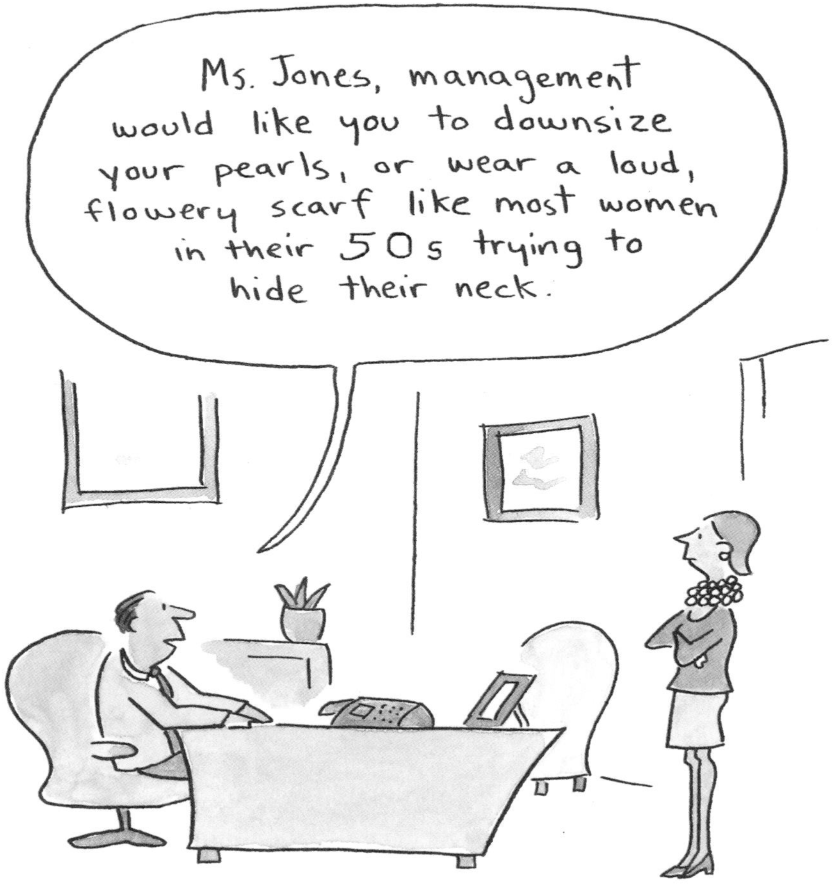
Ms. Jones, management would like you to downsize your pearls, or wear a loud, flowery scarf like most women in their 50s trying to hide their neck.

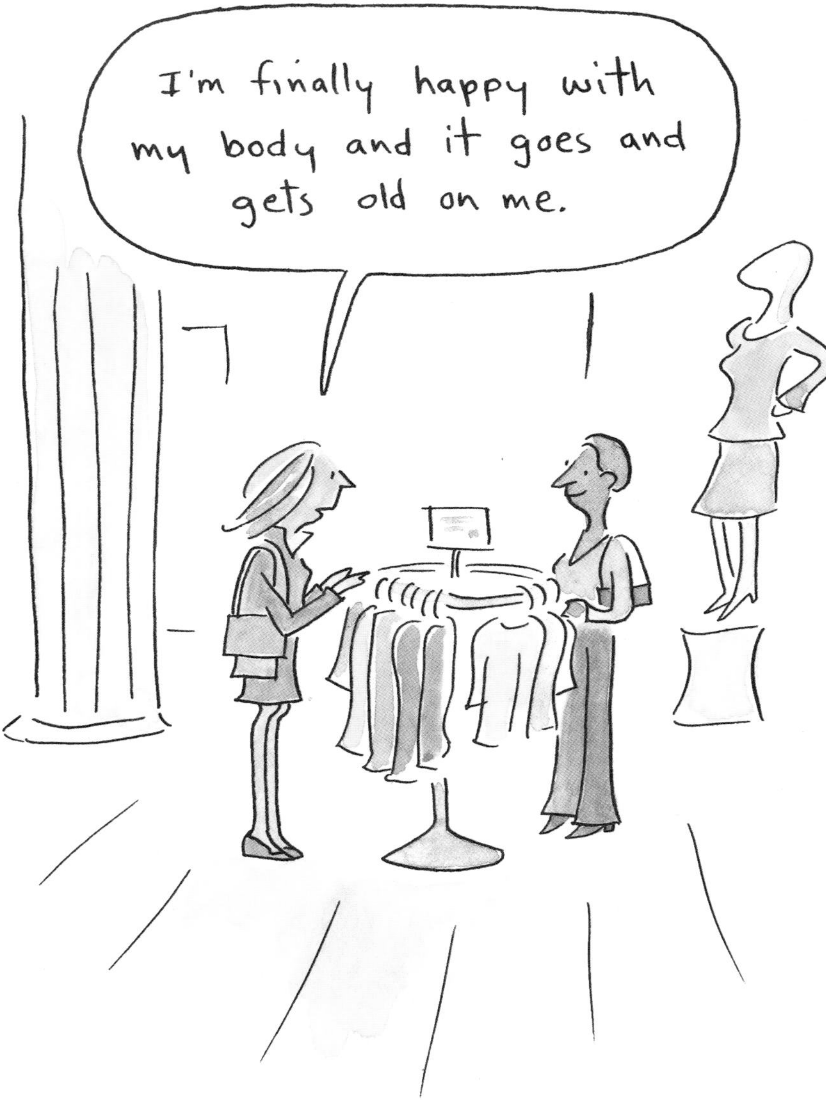
I'm finally happy with my body and it goes and gets old on me.

Pesky Produce

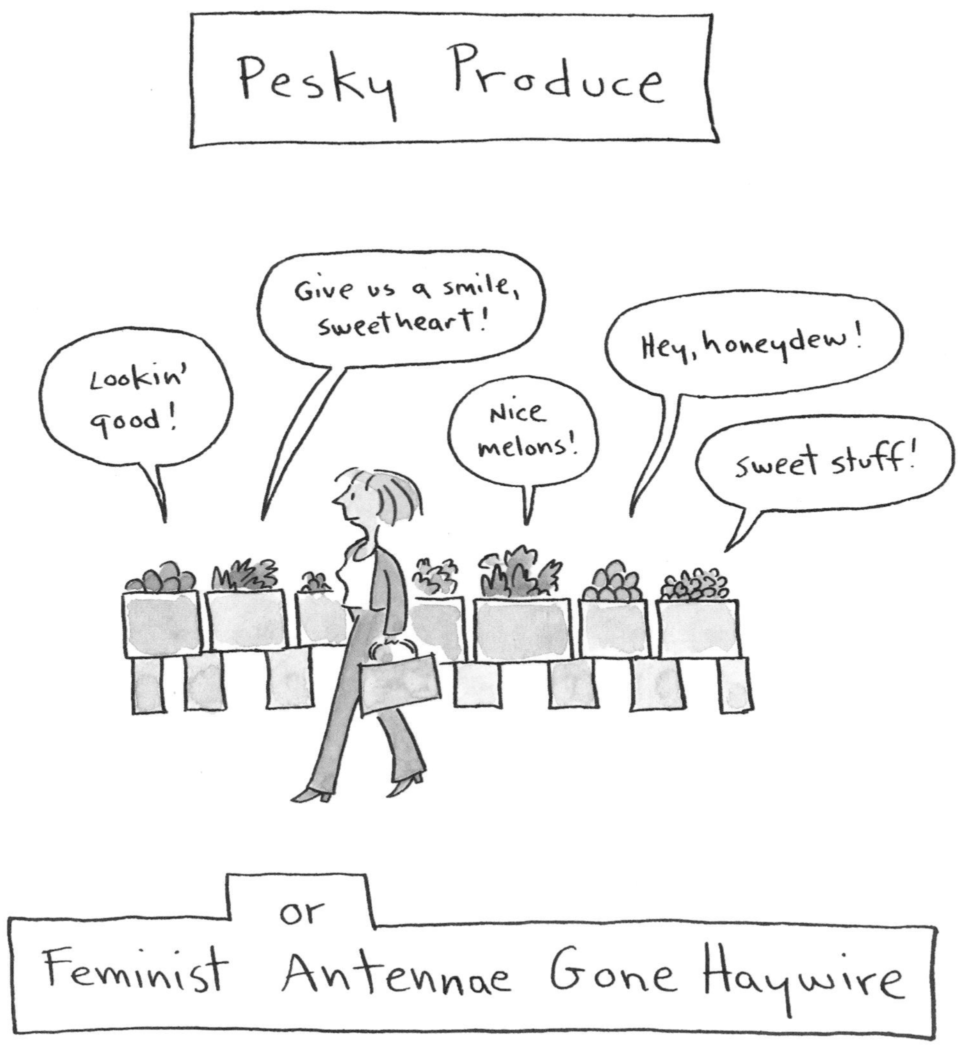
Lookin' good!
Give us a smile, sweetheart!
Nice melons!
Hey, honeydew!
Sweet stuff!

or

Feminist Antennae Gone Haywire

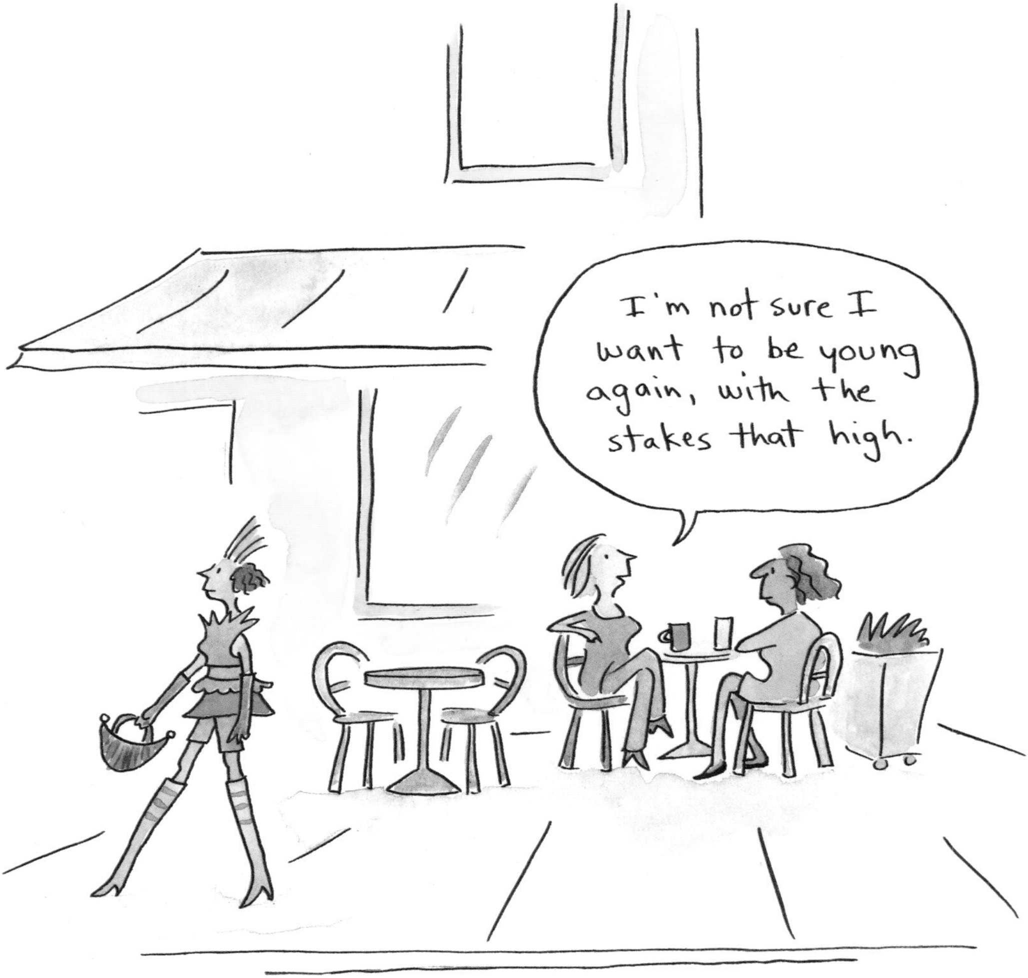
I'm not sure I want to be young again, with the stakes that high.

Rebellious Body Parts

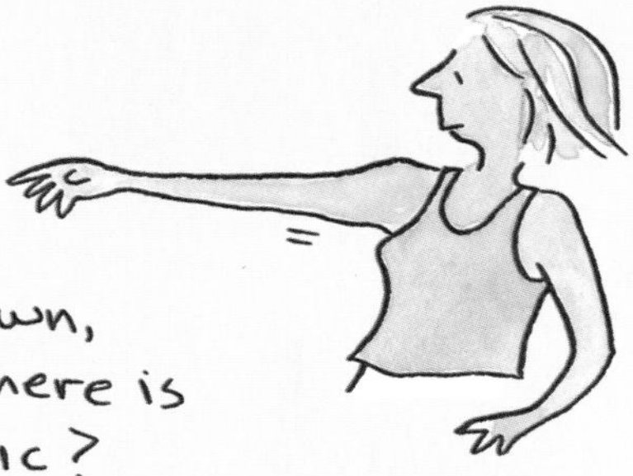

Does your upper arm have a mind of its own, dancing when there is no music?

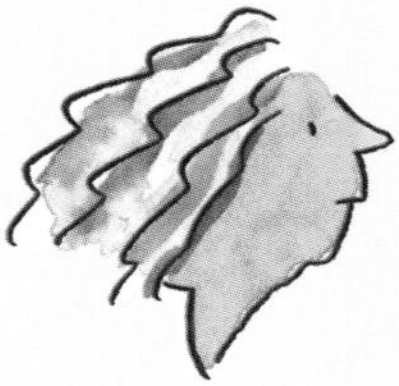

Does your chin have no confidence, falling down on a daily basis?

Do your heels need a drink (more than you do)?

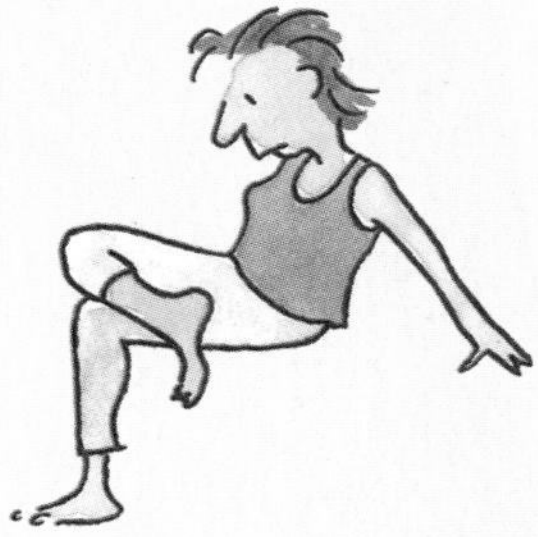

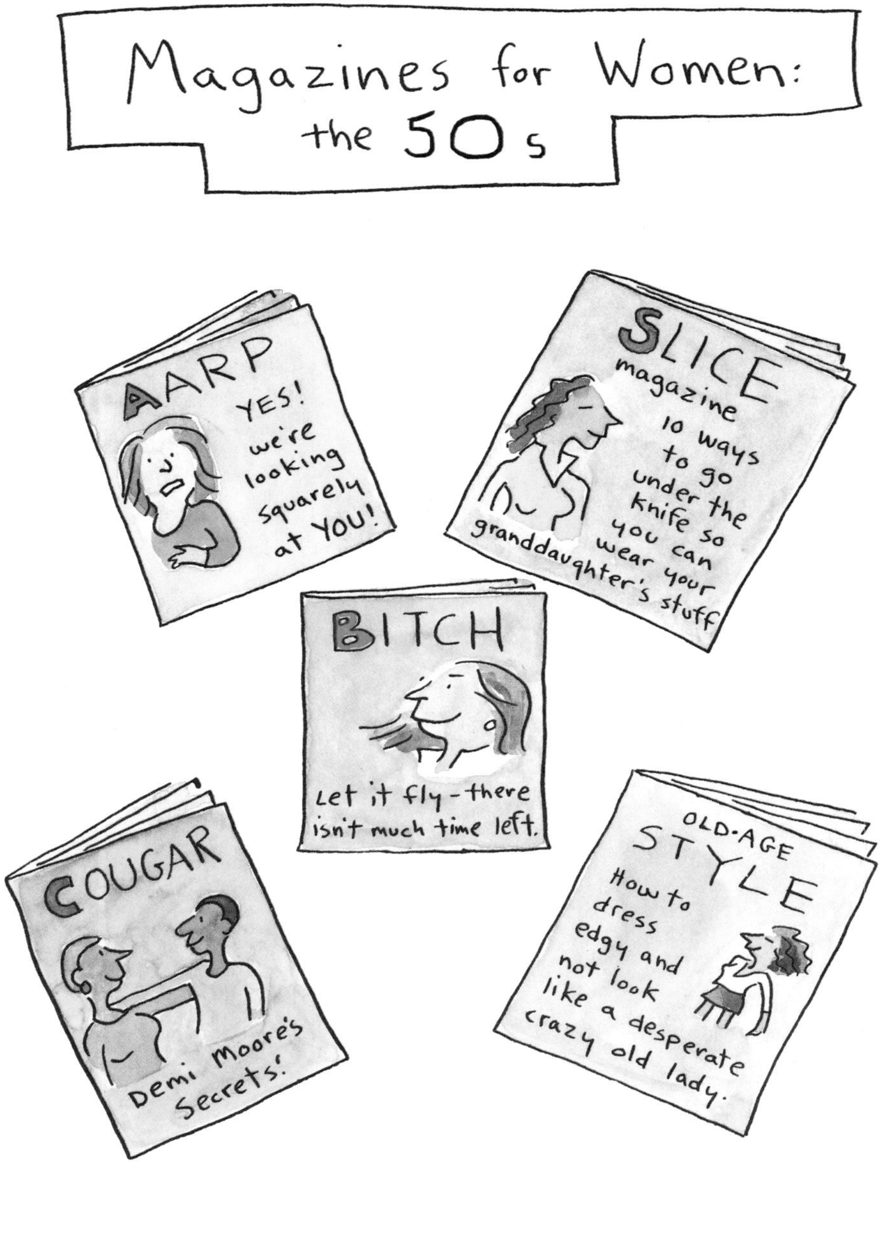

Magazines for Women: the 50s
AARP
YES! we're looking squarely at YOU!
SLICE magazine
10 ways to go under the knife so you can wear your granddaughter's stuff
BITCH
Let it fly - there isn't much time left.
COUGAR
Demi Moore's Secrets!
OLD-AGE STYLE
How to dress edgy and not look like a desperate crazy old lady.

Dangers of Dating Younger

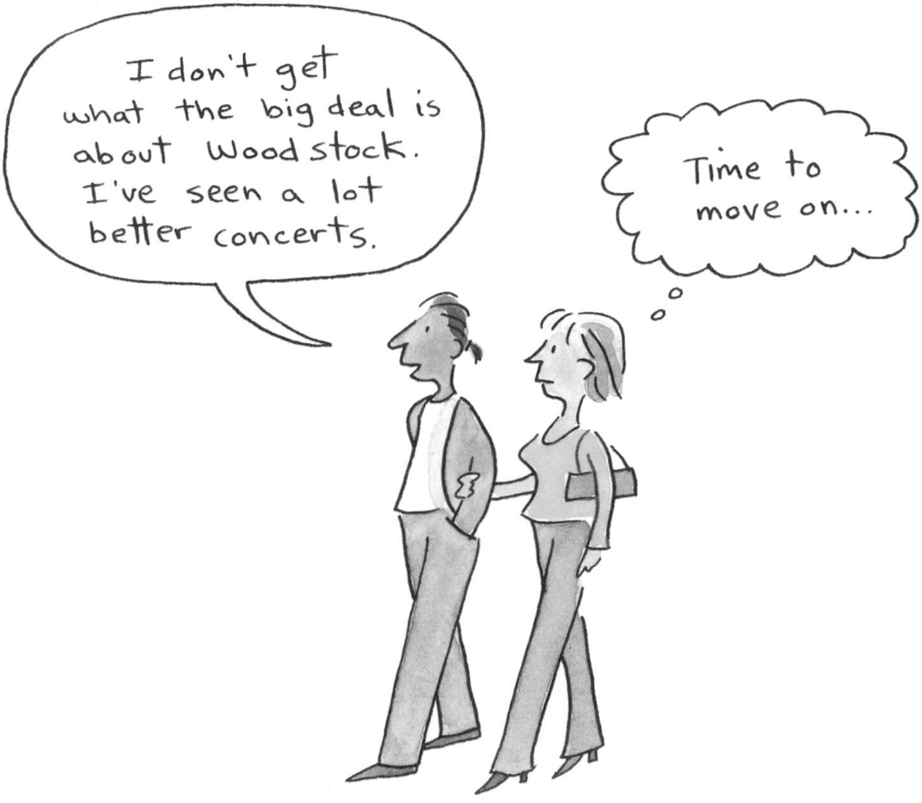
I don't get what the big deal is about Woodstock. I've seen a lot better concerts.
Time to move on...

Noncommittal Men

He won't commit to doing what you want now that there's so much free time.

hot dogs
football
dick flick
sex this way
quiche
baseball
chick flick
sex that way

OR

trying new things.

UGANDAN FOOD

THIS was NOT supposed to HAPPEN to ME

one morning you woke up..

AARGH! WHO IS THAT OLD LADY?!

So you avoid mirrors and live in a fantasy world where you are still 26.

Top 10 Reasons
to
Lie About your Age

1. It's fun to fool people.
2. Your clothes aren't aging.
3. No one will notice anyway.
4. Your boyfriend is young.
5. Your boyfriend is old.
6. Your dog won't tell.
7. Age brings respect.

8. You loved being 52.
9. You're tired of being carded.
10. No one believes you're a grandmother.

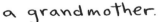

You're 50, you meet a 30-year-old guy. He's interested. You:

1. Hug him and don't let go

2. Run away

3. Tell him your inner mother is not available

4. Tell him your inner everything else is available

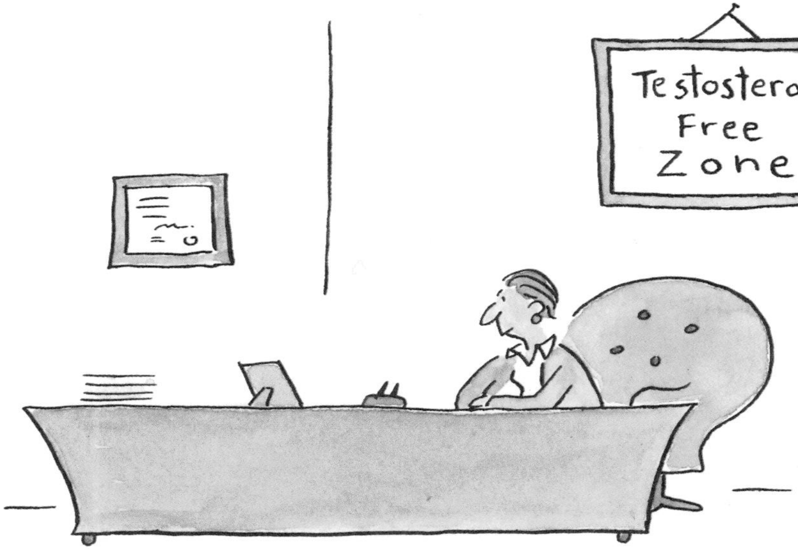
Testosterone
Free
Zone

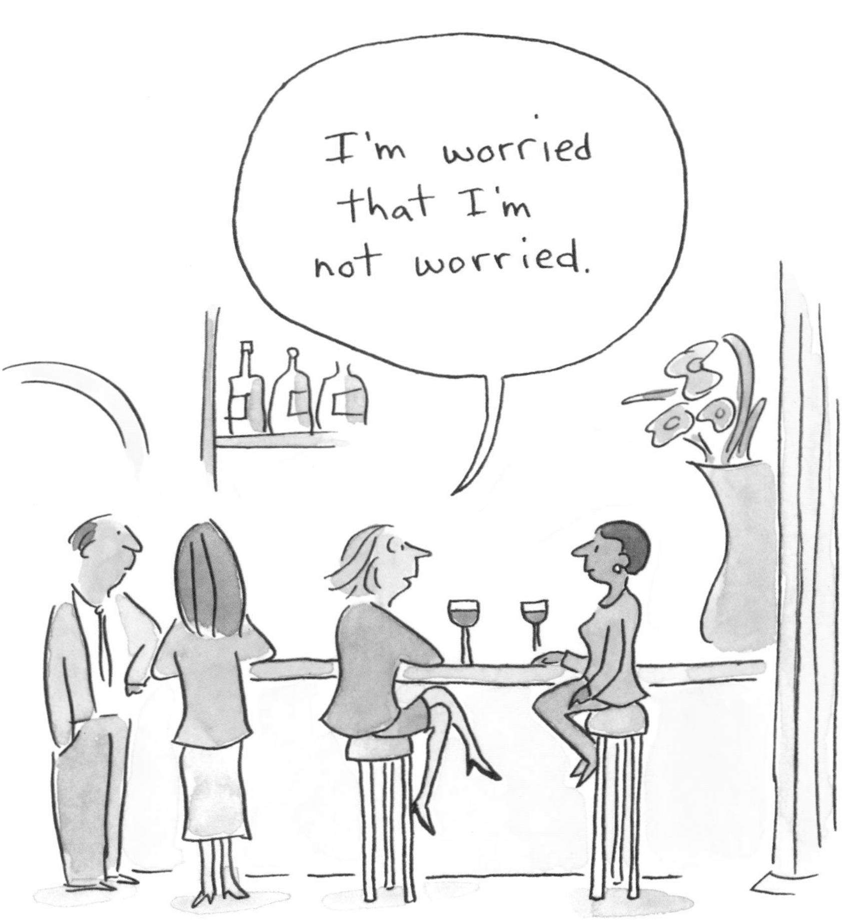
I'm worried that I'm not worried.

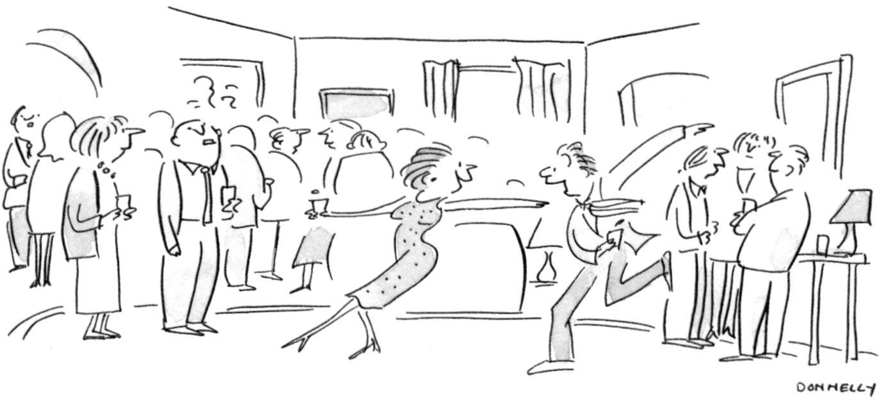
DONNELLY

"I hear their marriage is in trouble."

CHAPTER 6

60s
and beyond

I don't know if women in their 20s look at women in their 40s and think, that's what I want to be. I know I didn't. But now, in my 50s, my body is already telling me that I'm headed that way. One day, your knees are aching and wonder why: Oh, I am older, maybe *that's* why. In my mind, I'm 26, but my body tells me otherwise.

So I find myself seeking out women in their 60s and 70s, searching for role models. What part of me will sag? Will I wear long flowing gray hair, or short sassy white hair? I would like to look like Meryl Streep or Glenn Close—or even Whoopi Goldberg, but I think looking like her is a stretch. But I can model her attitude and spirit. You can't find that in a cream application. Growing up, the women I was fascinated with seemed to be full of life: my mother, Aunt Helen, my grandmother. They tried to be themselves in a world that often wouldn't let them. There weren't any women cartoonists to emulate, but two women writer friends of my family—Lucy Fletcher and Andy Logan—showed me that it was possible to be yourself creatively.

You don't need a mirror. I threw out the scale years ago, and now I want to toss the mirror. But I don't need to. Although it has taken me fifty years, I know who I am now, wrinkles and all. The mirror doesn't lie, but it can't tell me everything.

GIRLS NIGHT OUT

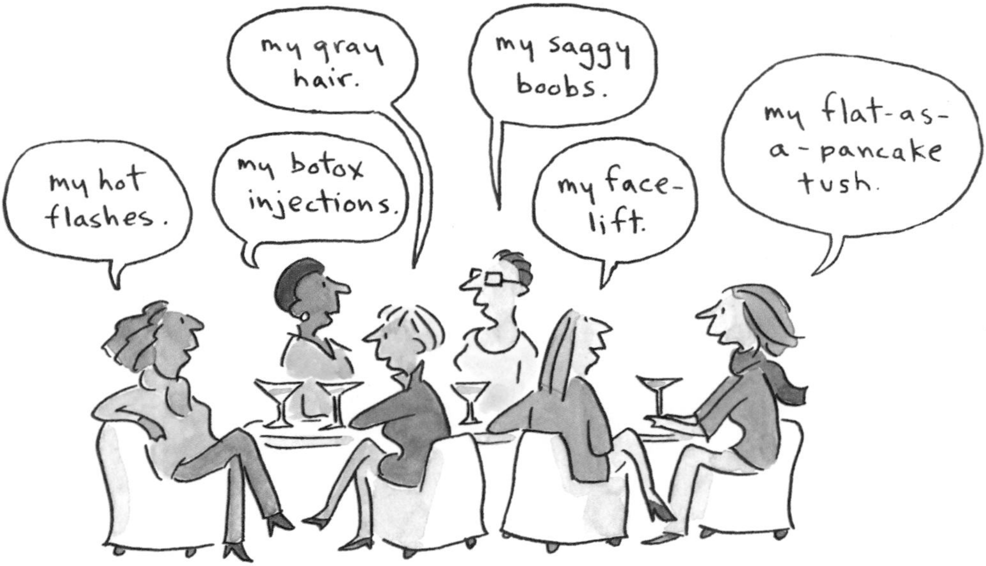
my hot flashes.
my gray hair.
my botox injections.
my saggy boobs.
my face-lift.
my flat-as-a-pancake tush.

If you look like this in your 60s, people will assume...

- You never left Vermont

- You love your garden and 23 grandkids

- You're nuts

- You have no real brains, just "intuition"

- You do yoga + crystals

Remember when "old" meant
blue hair, sensible shoes
and matching shifts
(and earrings, brooch,
and hand bag)?
(some states still have those)

NO MORE

Now you can aspire to be:

face-lifted, lipo-
suctioned, botoxed
bombshell.

Eileen fisher-
clad, heavy
makeup-ed
"individualist."

Leather-skinned,
makeup-less
biker chick.

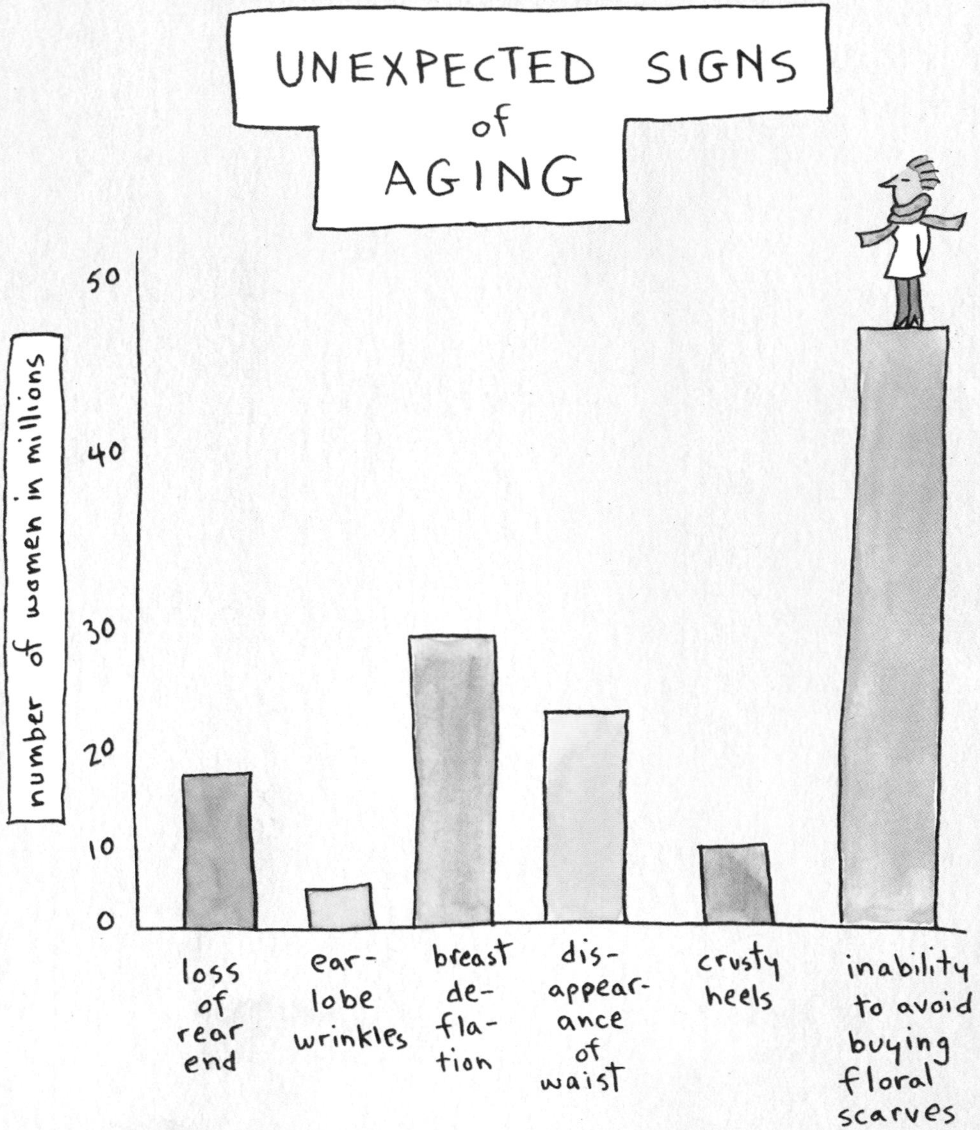
UNEXPECTED SIGNS of AGING
number of women in millions
50
40
30
20
10
0
loss of rear end
ear-lobe wrinkles
breast de-fla-tion
dis-appear-ance of waist
crusty heels
inability to avoid buying floral scarves

It seemed simple then, you were
either/or. Now there are
many ways to be older.
Some of my favorites:

meryl streep-type

Whoopi
Goldberg-girl

Hillary
Clinton-cutie

Yoko Ono-cool

Susan Sarandon-Sultry

Rebellious Body Parts

Do your laugh lines want to stick around permanently?

No matter how many crunches applied, your stomach muscles are staging a sit-down strike?

And remember that rear end you loved to hate?
GONE.
(now you want it back, right?)

Menopause Basics

Dont announce your hot flashes to the world.

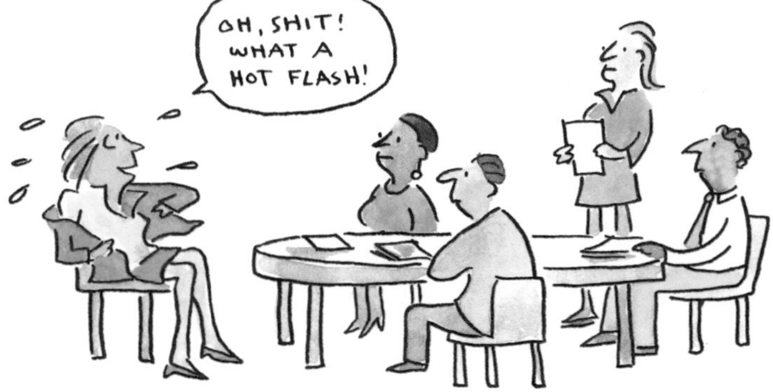
OH, SHIT! WHAT A HOT FLASH!

Be careful how much you take off during hot flashes.

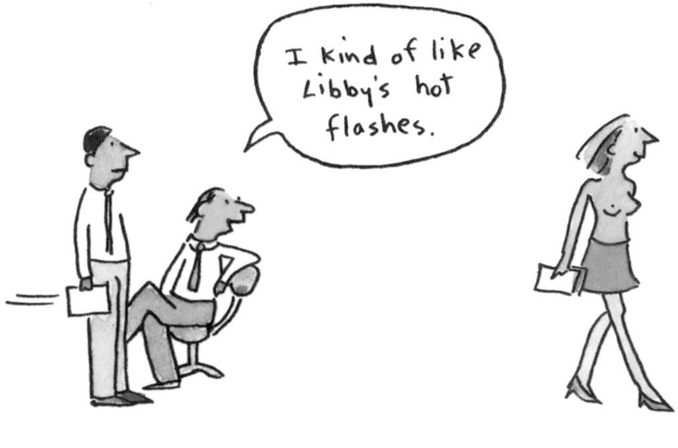
I kind of like Libby's hot flashes.

Don't knock your boss over running to pee.

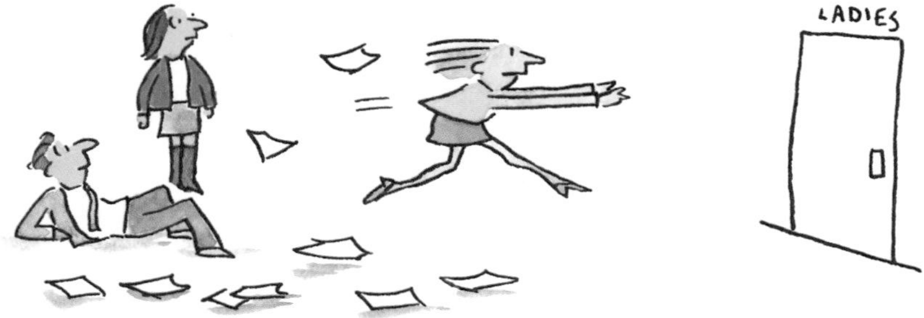
LADIES

Buy stock in vaginal lubricant if you actually want to have sex.

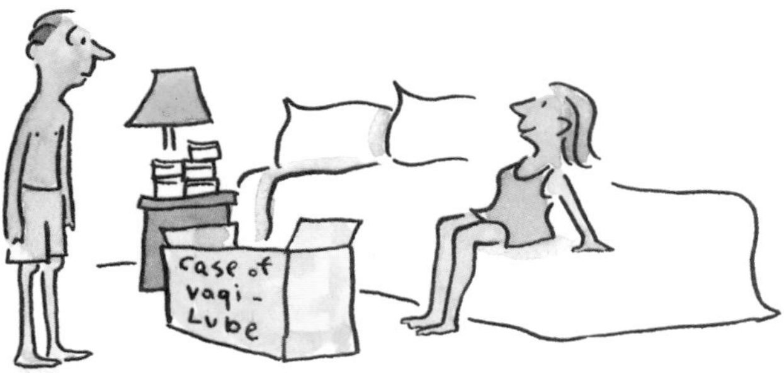
case of vagi-Lube

How NOT to get sucked into feeling old.

seat, ma'am?
No, thanks.
what are you nuts? Not old!
stupid kid.

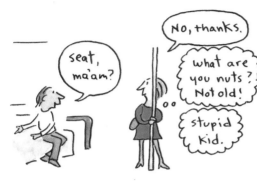

1. Don't take seat on bus.

I had so many lovers, I can't remember them all.

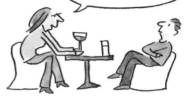

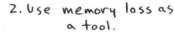

2. Use memory loss as a tool.

He looks pretty good when he's fuzzy.
Even looks like he has hair.

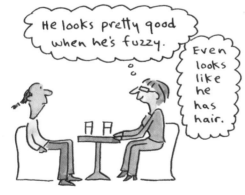

3. wear your reading glasses all the time during a bad date.

I hope they appreciate this

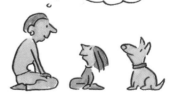

4. Get down on the floor with kids + dogs.

Yippee! Another day to find wrinkles + gray!

5. wake up happy.

I'm not as bad off as her.

6. Go skinny dipping.

I can't remember.
who cares!

7. Go with the flow.

8. throw out AARP mail.

May I help you, Miss?
Thanks for calling me Miss!
want $10?

9. Reward thoughtful youngsters.

HOW to LOOK SEXY at 60

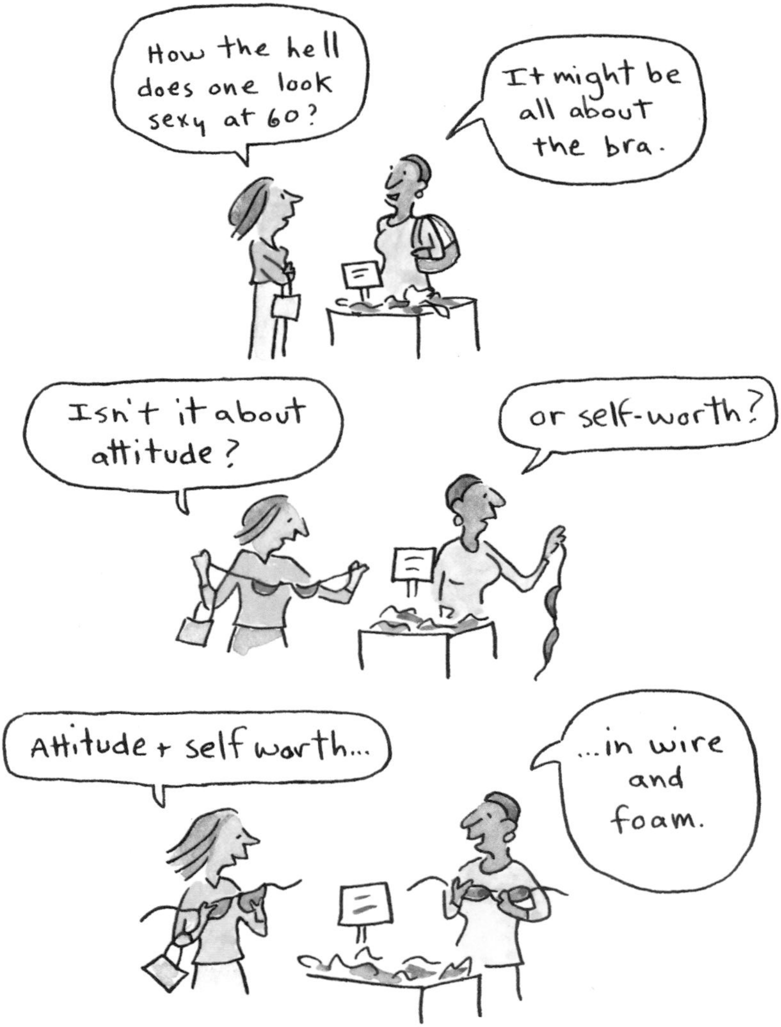
How the hell does one look sexy at 60?
It might be all about the bra.
Isn't it about attitude?
or self-worth?
Attitude + self worth...
...in wire and foam.

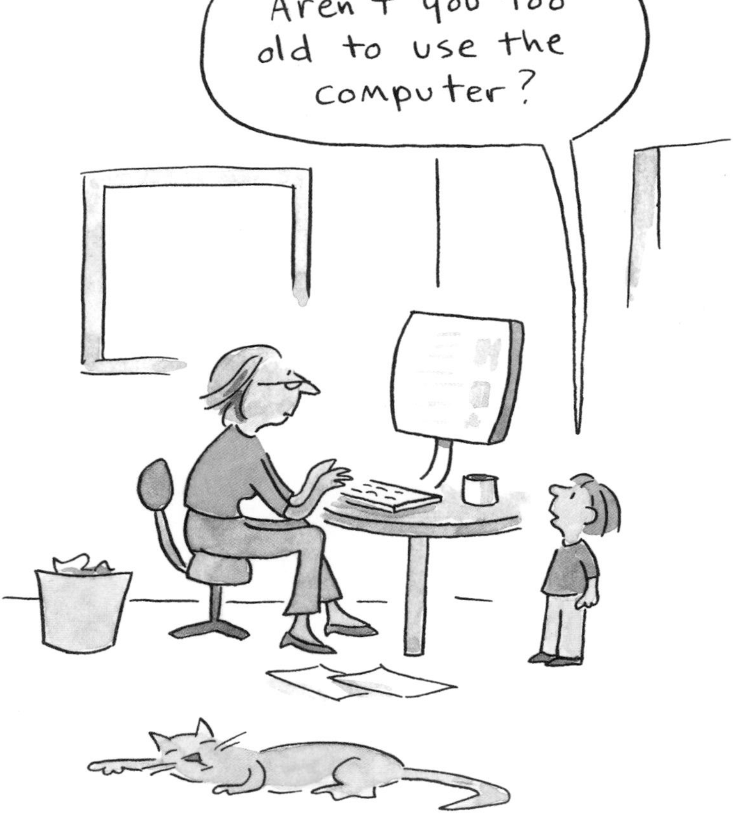
Aren't you too old to use the computer?

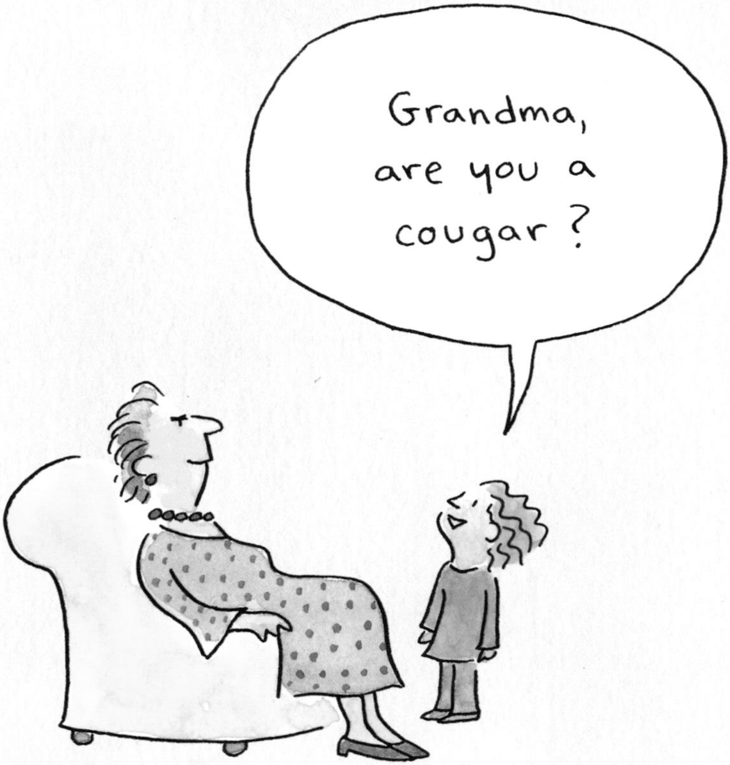
Grandma, are you a cougar?

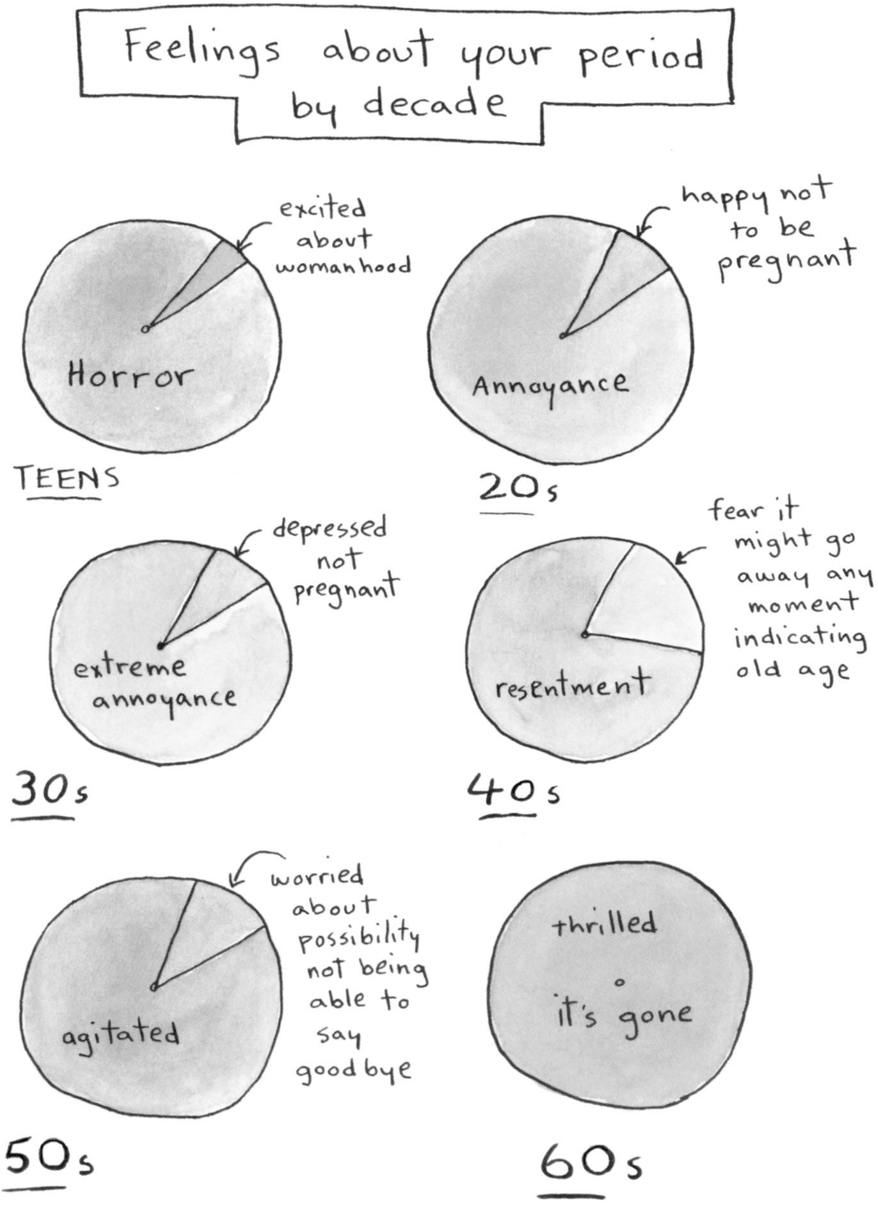
Feelings about your period by decade
excited about womanhood
Horror
TEENS
happy not to be pregnant
Annoyance
20s
depressed not pregnant
extreme annoyance
30s
fear it might go away any moment indicating old age
resentment
40s
worried about possibility not being able to say goodbye
agitated
50s
thrilled
it's gone
60s

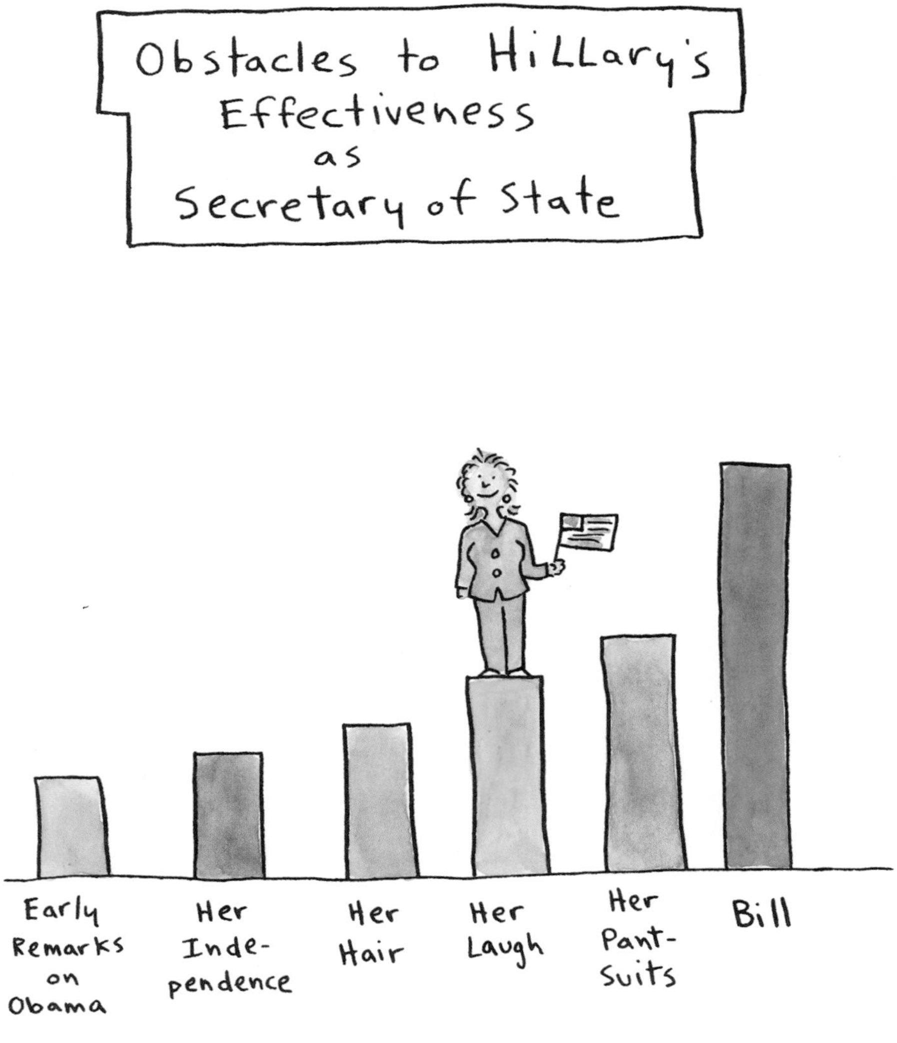
Obstacles to HiLLary's Effectiveness as Secretary of State
Early Remarks on Obama
Her Inde-pendence
Her Hair
Her Laugh
Her Pant-Suits
Bill

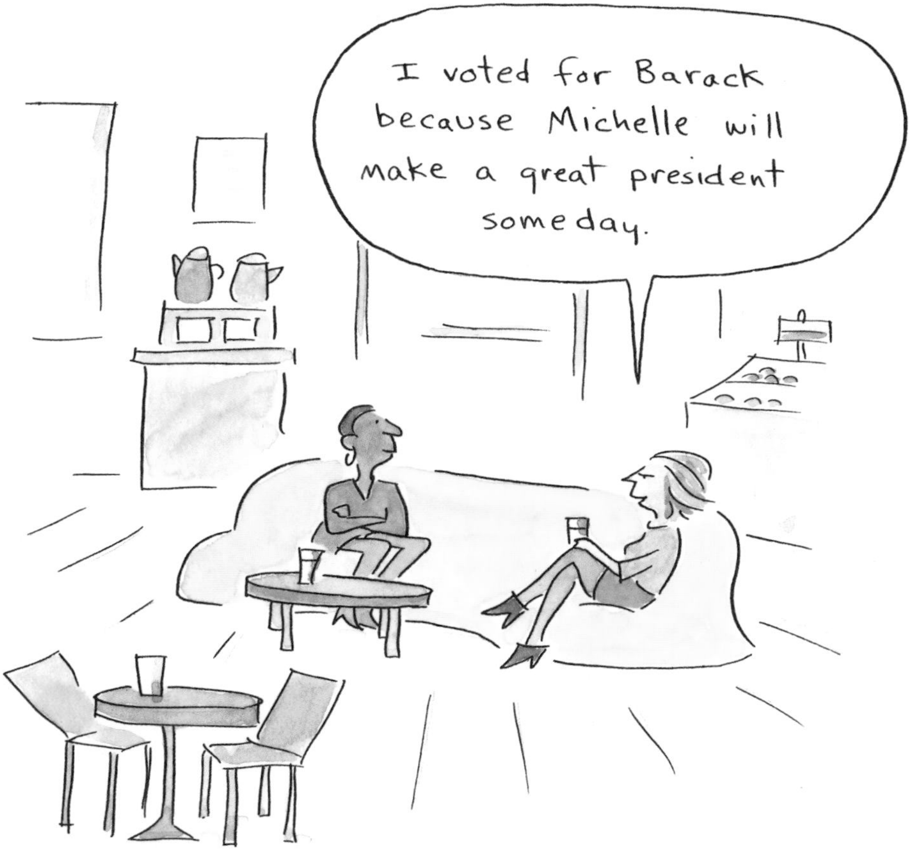
I voted for Barack because Michelle will make a great president someday.

MAGAZINES for WOMEN: the 60s

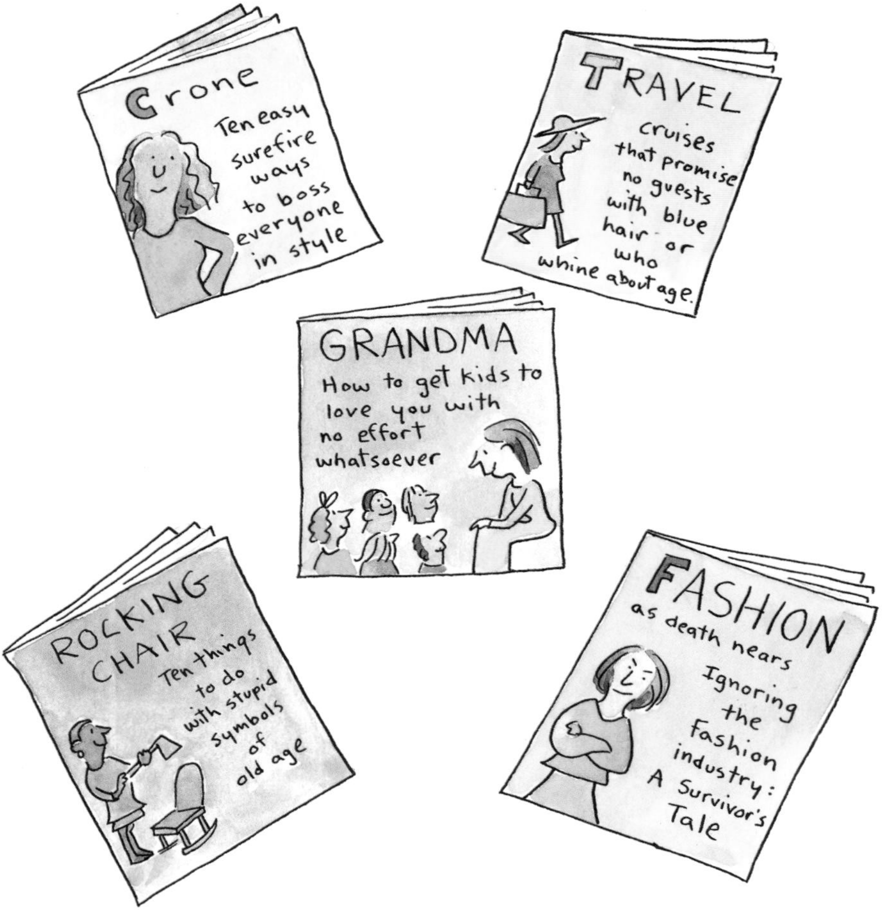
Crone
Ten easy surefire ways to boss everyone in style
TRAVEL
cruises that promise no guests with blue hair or who whine about age.
GRANDMA
How to get kids to love you with no effort whatsoever
ROCKING CHAIR
Ten things to do with stupid symbols of old age
FASHION
as death nears
Ignoring the fashion industry: A Survivor's Tale

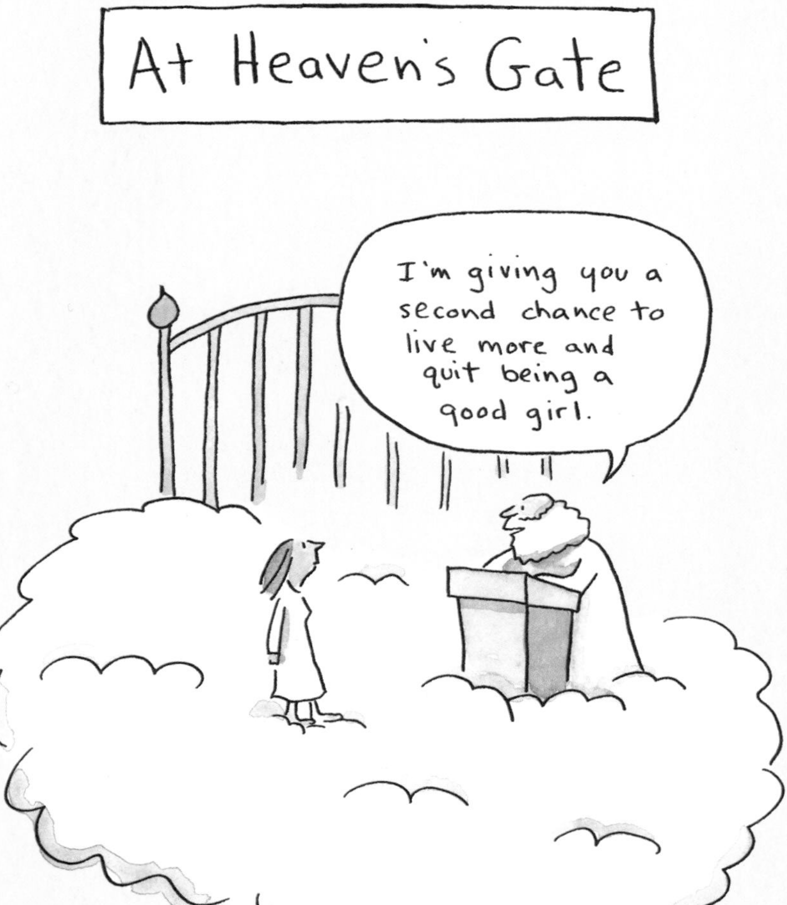
At Heaven's Gate
I'm giving you a second chance to live more and quit being a good girl.

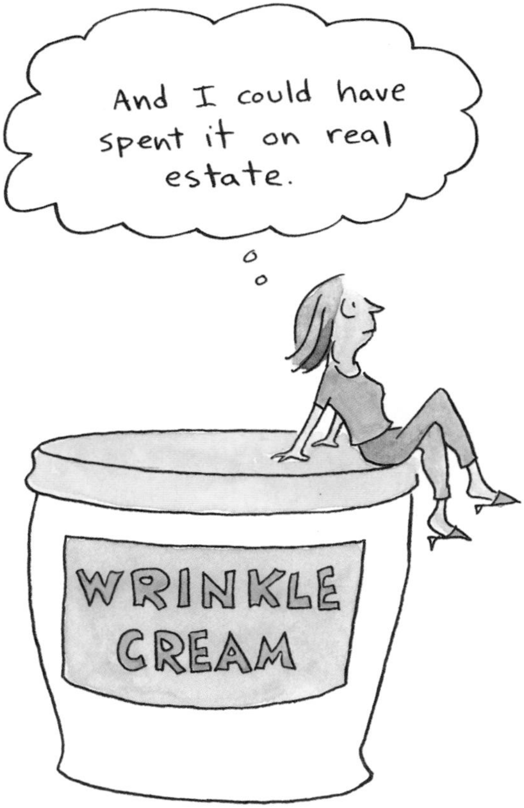
And I could have spent it on real estate.
WRINKLE CREAM

Amount of face product used in one year by a postmenopausal woman.

Noncommittal Men

He won't commit to leaving you alone.

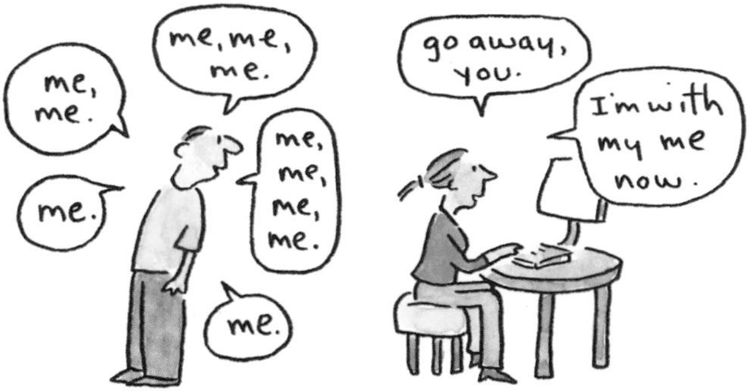
me, me.
me, me, me.
me.
me, me, me, me.
me.
go away, you.
I'm with my me now.

or
to joining your feminist book group.

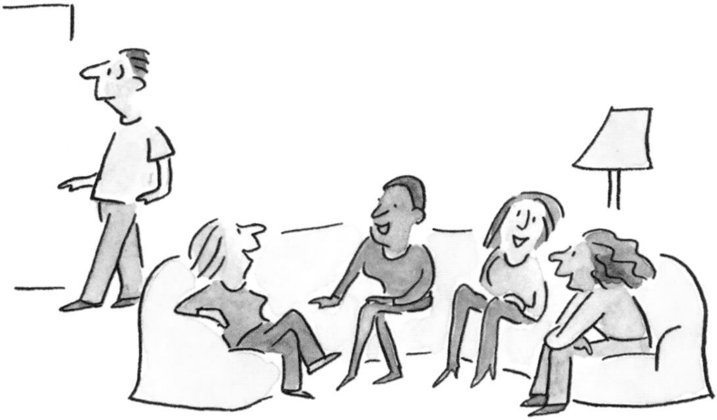

PERKS of OLD AGE

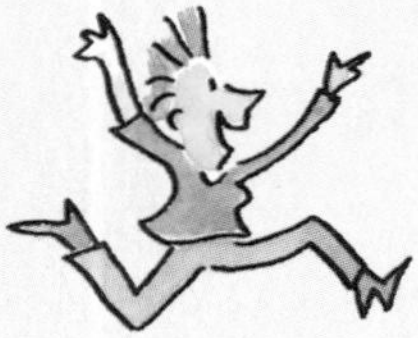

no period.

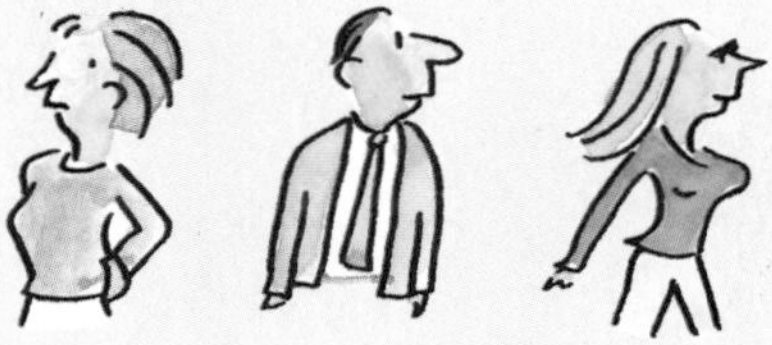

no stares from men.

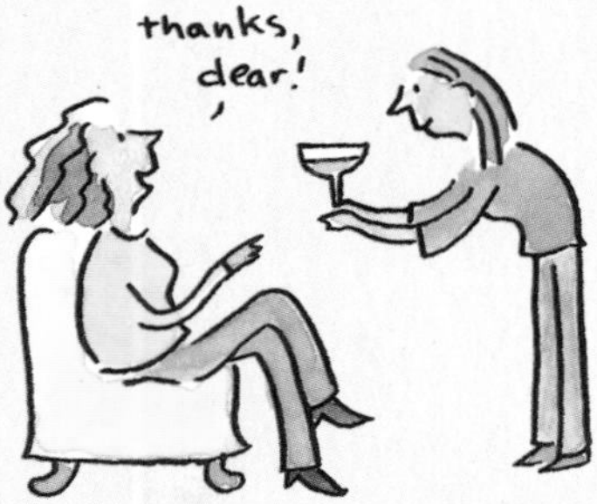
thanks, dear!

getting waited on.

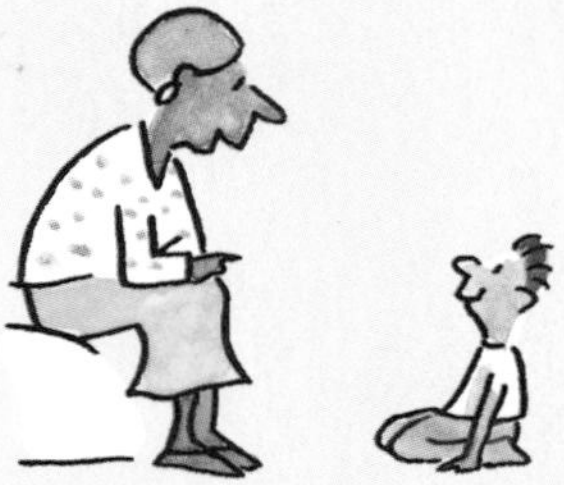

people listen.

Age brings Great Wisdom

Black goes with everything.

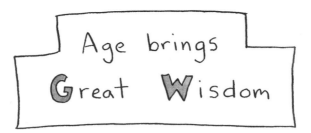

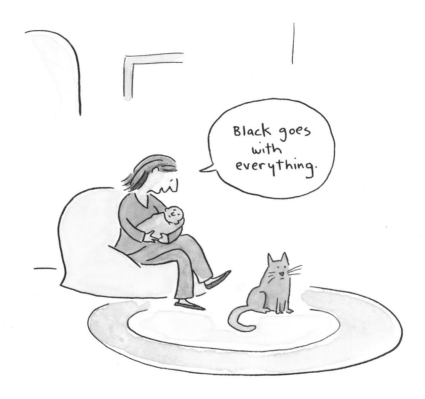

Sagging Breasts

It's a slow descent.
One day, you realize that your beloved breasts are hanging out down with your navel.

What
to do?

Lop them off and get new ones?

BOOB STORE

Camp out at Victoria's secret until you find the right one.

Throw away your bras and wear really baggy clothes. Pretend you don't care.

Put props under them.

Inflate them.

BIKE PUMP

Sex in your 60s

no contraception

no inhibition

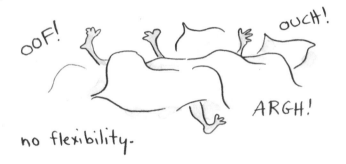

OOF!

OUCH!

ARGH!

no flexibility.

It's all about slowly letting go.

say what you want:

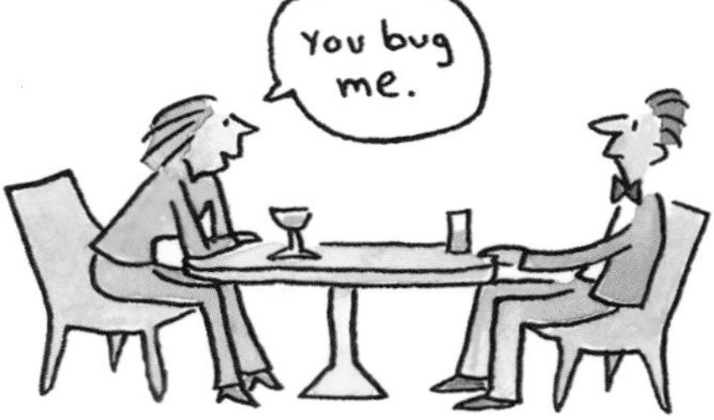
You bug me.

do what you want:

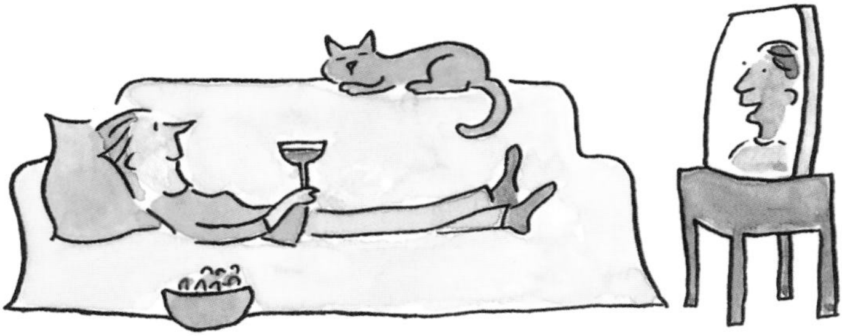

acknowledgments

As if my life depends on it, I watch and listen to the women in my life: my mother, grandmothers, stepmother, mother-in-law, sisters, daughters, and girlfriends, and I thank them for being my muses. I would like to thank my agent, David Kuhn, for his ability to listen, guide, and be enthusiastic for my (almost) every idea; as an agent, they don't get any better. I am grateful to my editors and the designers at Chronicle for helping me visualize and execute my vision. The seed for this book emerged at the suggestion of my supportive editor at www.wowowow.com, Joni Evans, and was fed with inspiration as I taught my wonderful Women's Studies students at Vassar. There aren't enough ways to thank Roz Chast for her wonderful introduction and her dear friendship (through all the womanly and cartoony rights of passage). My biggest thanks goes to my feminist husband, Michael, who is my sounding board and best friend; and to our two daughters, Ella and Gretchen, who provided me with inspiration, guidance, and love.

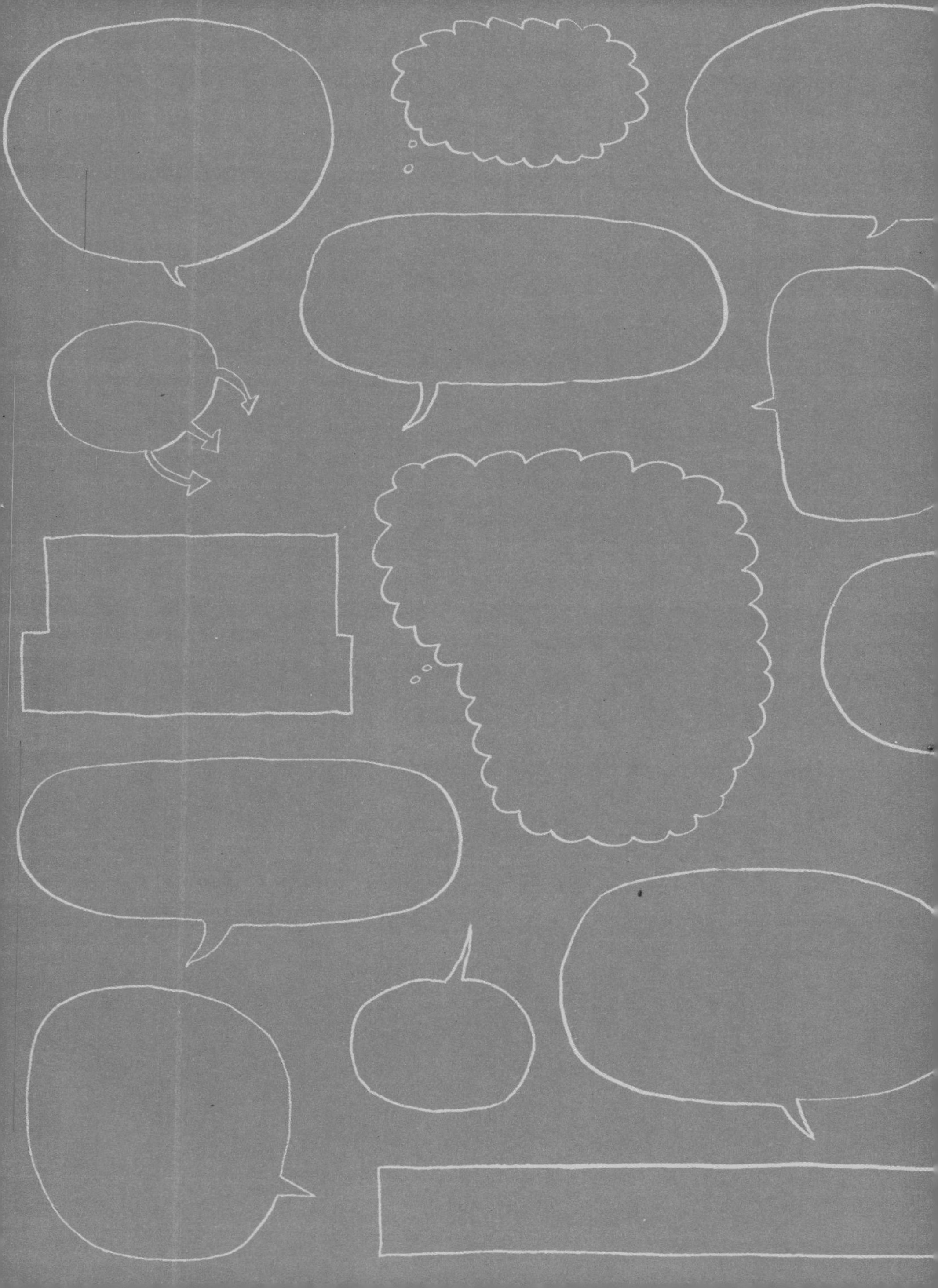